THE A-Z OF
BEHAVING
BADLY

THE A-Z OF BEHAVING BADLY

WRITTEN BY

SIMON NYE and PAUL DORNAN

EDITED BY
ELAINE CAMERON

PAVILION

ACKNOWLEDGEMENTS

The authors reluctantly thank the following:
Beryl Vertue, Executive Producer with Special Responsibility for
Good Taste and Decency, laughably.
Jay Maidment, probably some mincing queen with an old Instamatic
and discount card for Snappy Snaps.
Chris Dymond and the rest of his infant class for various cutting
and pasting skills.
Trevor Dolby, man in a dazzling white shirt and tie who allegedly
played some sort of coordinating role.
And finally
Martin Clunes and Neil Morrissey whose
outrageous behaviour at editorial
meetings was immensely saddening.

First published in Great Britain in 1995 by
Pavilion Books Limited
26 Upper Ground
London SE1 9PD

Copyright Simon Nye/Hartswood Films/Pavilion Books
The moral rights of the copyright holders have been asserted

Special photography Jay Maidment

Designed and artworked by the Bridgewater Book Company
Chris Dymond/Glyn Bridgewater/Ian Roberts

With thanks for additional material to
Mike Barfield
Will Buckley
Simon Goodman
Jeremy Glover
Tim Beckerley
Salv Scimone
Nick Hildred
Jed Parsons
Ludwig Adler

The publishers wish to thank Stella Artois

A CIP catalogue record for this book
is available from the British Library.

ISBN 1-85793-801-1

Printed and bound in Great Britain by Butler and Tanner.

24681097531

This book may be ordered by post direct from the publisher. Please
contact the Marketing Department. But try your bookshop first.

INTRODUCTION

One evening we are minding our own business in the pub when a top London publisher puts down his sherry, shuffles up to us and, dribbling slightly, asks us if we want to write a manual of Bad Behaviour. Wondering why we of all people should be picked, we stop pogoing to Crazy Horses, climb back into our pants and wait for him to offer us a pitcher of the week's guest lager, a light hoppy Norwegian brew called Boff.

Writing a book is not something you rush into, especially if the last book you read all the way through was The Kate Bush Story, and that was in 1989. So we got hold of a list of authors, rang them up and asked them how much of a bitch it was to write one. The answers varied from "Who the hell gave you my number?" and "Whatever you do, don't sign any-thing with Pavilion Books" to "You'll spend six months of your life on it and at the end of the day the stocking-filler they'll be buying is the Have I Got News For You book." A lot of writers were unavailable for comment. Martin Amis was out buying a magazine, Jilly Cooper had gone into Stroud to get her car serviced and Salman Rushdie was busy rustling up a bit of lunch for his bodyguards.

We've plunged in anyway. We can't pretend it was hard work. When your philosophy of life is as fully developed and coher-ent as ours is, you don't need to ponce around too much bas-ically. Occasionally there were frictions between us leading to fist-fights which sometimes spilled out onto the street and we had to be separated by pedestrians. Slanging matches with the design team became everyday occurrences when they refused to use admittedly racey photos from our private collection. Some pages, obviously, are little short of complete gibberish

But we're proud of it. The book is many things - it's a treasure trove of ideas, it's a glimpse into our world and, last but not least, it's actually a laugh-out-loud comedy event. The words definitive and publishing sensation hover around it like housemartins.

Buy it, or we'll come round to your house, sit on your sofa and talk to you.

(Just in case you are in the shop making up your mind whether to buy this book or not).

M ATES

Let's face it, nothing but nothing is more important to the modern man than his mates. Indeed it's no exaggeration to say that we believe that having good mates are really what makes the world go round, what really makes a man's life worth living. Certainly a man can't really even begin to Behave Badly without at least one mate at his side. For as the good book says a man can have all the material, sporting and job success that he likes, all the beautiful young birds flocking to his bed at all hours of the day and night, yea he can even have the latest Audi Quatro Automatic soft top with dual airbags but if he has not mates to envy him and take the piss out of him then he is but an empty bell tolling in a hollow room.

In fact we both feel so strongly about matedom that we were up till four in the morning last night working on the first ever Mates Charter, a sacred document that we wrote on the back of an old 30 yards backstroke swimming certificate. Why not copy it out in neat yourself and get your mates to sign it ??? Well. Have you??

MATES CHARTER

1 I totally and utterly agree that mates are the most important thing in the world - except for our quite reasonable dreams
that one day we will get to spend of delirious sexual abandon
either with Kylie or the girl who plays Nicole in Clio advert.

2 I believe mates should stand by each other at all times
and in all circumstances, though I do recognise this might be
a bit of a problem if our mate insists on starting a scrap
with thirty Welsh squaddies after a rugby international.

3 I agree mates have the following obligations and duties:
a) Going out for a Quiet Drink. This should hold true at all
times, especially during the week or on a slack tele night.
Neither mate must or should be made to feel like a sad for
doing so and/or for not having any other friends to go out
with.
b) Rubbernecking at Girls. This should happen at all times
when mates are together in a public place. All such leering
should be as wide-ranging as possible and include full allow-
ances for differences of sexual taste and experience.
Phrases such as "Watch out. Here comes your kind of trouble"
are a true sign of proper matedom in action.
c) Emotional Support. Mates should be there for one another
at moments of intense emotional crises such as England v New
Zealand in the Rugby World Cup.
d) Lying to Girlfriends. including full whereabouts cover
story services and instant re-writing of sexual history if
and when required.
e) Mutual Back Slapping. Though mates may take the piss out
of one another in private, doing so in public, especially in
front of fanciable girls, is expressly forbidden, unless the
humour is of the gentle, appreciative kind that builds up
the image of both parties in the eyes of all would-be sex
partners.

4 On the other hand I wholly agree that mates do not have to:
a) Like your clothes
b) Take your new hair cut seriously
c) Agree with anything you say especially when it comes to
music and the question of the relative legacies of punk and
Motown on contemporary pop
d) Pretend they don't fancy your new girlfriend
e) Pretend they do fancy your new girlfriend
f) Like or even talk to your new girlfriend unless they do
fancy them a little bit
g) Clean up your vomit after you unless they themselves have
caused it
h) Watch each other cry, unless it's in the unlikely event of
England winning the football, rugby or cricket world cups or
Sonia proving what a plucky scouse trooper she really is and
storming it in the Eurovision Song Contest.

5 I agree that my mate may call attention to any breach of
the above conditions either deliberate or accidental at any
time by use of the word 'WANKER' and/or physical violence of
a medium to extreme nature.

All of the conditions hereinunder are fully binding at all
times without undue prejudice. whatever that means.
Yours sincerely,

. . . .
YOU

. . . .
YOUR MATE

10 Sleep your way around a map of Britain

9 Stop being taken in by ads in the newspaper for X-ray Specs that just DO NOT WORK

8 At least try not to snigger when someone says "Are you coming?"

7 Score spectacular winning try in England rugby grand slam

6 Get into a nightclub without begging or bribing the bouncer

5 Sleep your way around a map of Europe

4 Have plaster cast made of your genitals in their prime to admire in lonely withered old age

3 Find half-way convincing answer to the question: "What is it about men and blondes with big tits?"

2 Write best-selling first novel that becomes philosphical bible of a generation of young girl students

1 Sleep your way around a map of the world

E BIG THREE-O   For Girls

'30' figures highly in the Demonology of Bad Behaviour. Not only is it a really boring speed limit, but it's the age around which most previously normal birds start to live, sleep, dream and eat baby (not literally eat baby - that would be wrong).

If they don't actually want one right now this minute, in their heads they're already drawing up fantastically strict timetables: If we start next August Bank Holiday, allow the statistically average eight and a half months to conceive, factoring in his family history of miserably low sperm counts, so call it eleven months, add nine...

Soon your totty's biological clock is ticking away so loudly you can't hear the TV with her sitting next to you unless you wrap her in a blanket and lag her with cushions. Some blokes decide that yes, they would like kids, if only because it's nice to have someone to talk to you when you're old. But if you like your eggs unfertilised, you better bale out when your bird shows the following warning signs:

1. Takes notes in a little red notebook during disposable nappy adverts.

2. Apropos of nothing, tells you "You'd make a good father," but in an odd voice that sounds as if they don't quite believe it.

3. Browsing around her flat one day, you find a bit of scrap-paper with her first name and your surname written all over it in her hand-writing, as well as one bit where she's put her first name but the surname of your best friend.

4. Starts buying you giant underwear - huge, baggy boxer-shorts - because she read in 'Company' that it doesn't do for your nuts to get over-heated.

5. Gets drunk, climbs on the roof at two in the morning, and stands there shouting, 'I WANT BAAABBBYYY! I WANT BAAABBBYY!"

6. Leaves you for a younger bloke who's not afraid of committment.

NNOYING THINGS, TOP TEN

10 Shaving
9   People who do really good accents
8   The Radio 1 Roadshow
7   People who do really good impressions
6   'Controversial' newspaper columnists
5   Conceptual artists
4   People who do really bad accents/impressions
3   Caravans
2   People who don't do accents or impressions at all but are still funnier than you are
1   Keanu Reeves, obviously

BEAUFORT OFF-YOUR-FACE SCALE

The BEAUFORT SCALE measures Wind speed. (It goes from 0 to 12, e.g. 5 = fresh breeze: leaves flutter in trees; 10 = storm: hats blow off, etc.) But who cares these days about how fast wind is going? It's not interesting. The BEAUFORT SCALE is useful however, for describing how off-your-face you get during a night in the Dog & Video:

Beaufort number	Description of condition
0	Stone cold sober. Brain as sharp as an army bayonet.
1	Still sober. Pleasure senses activated. Feeling of well-being.
2	Lager warming up head. Crisps are ordered. Barmaid complimented on choice of blouse.
3	Crossword in newspaper is filled in. After a while blanks are filled with random letters and numbers.
4	Barmaid complimented on choice of bra, partially visible when bending to get packets of crisps. Try to instigate conversation about bras. Order half a dozen packets of crisps one by one.
5	Have brilliant discussion with bloke at bar. Devise fool-proof scheme for winning the lottery, sort out English tennis problems, agree that people are the same the world over except the bloody Japanese.
6	Feel like a demi-God. Map out rest of life on beer-mat. Realise that everybody loves you. Ring up parents to tell them you love them. Ring girlfriend to say you love her and she still has an amazing arse.
7	Send drinks over to woman sitting at table with boyfriend. No reaction. Scribble out message of love across five beer-mats and frisbee them to her across the room. Boyfriend asks you outside. You buy him a Slim Panatela.
8	Some slurring. Offer to buy drinks for everyone in room. Lots of people say yes. Go round bar hugging them one by one. Fall over. Get up. Go round pub hugging everyone again.
9	Head-ache kicks in. Pint tastes off. Send it back. Pint comes back tasting the same. Say "That's better, much better." Fight nausea by trying to play Pub Mastermind. Play for ten minutes before seeing 'Out of order' sign sello-taped to front.
10	Some doubling of vision. Stand on table shouting abuse at all four barmen. Talked down by barmen's wives, who you offer to give a baby to. Fall over. Get up. Fall over. Impale head on corner of table. Fail to notice oozing head wound.
11	Speech no longer possible. Eventually manage to find door. Sit and take stock. Realise you are sitting in pub cellar, having taken a wrong turning. In best Rod Stewart voice start to sing I am vomiting. Realise you are. Pass out.
12	Put in minicab by somebody. Give home address. Taken home. Can't get key in door. Realise you've given address of Arsenal Football Club and are trying to open door to West Stand. Generally pleased at way evening has gone. Pass out again.

BANK, sperm

NOW THAT'S WHAT YOU CALL A PART-TIME JOB.

BAYWATCH

Why it is unrealistic.

Although, in its own way, Baywatch is a thoroughly entertaining programme it does suffer from one fundamental flaw - there are no voyeurs. Week in, week out Pamela Anderson and friends strut their stuff down the beach and not once do you see a group of lads lying on their stomachs and copping a good, long letch.

Each episode would be much more realistic if, rather than having to sit through the increasingly dull musical interlude, we could watch them getting beered up and taking it in turns to make a pass at Pammy.

And every so often one of them would actually pork her or, at the very least, get a damn good feel. This would improve the programme by giving us characters we could identify with and generate a feel-good factor whenever our characters got lucky.

One for Mr Hasselhoff to think about.

BADLY BEHAVED HEROES

If you're in the public eye day after day you get slagged off a lot. Some people deserve it. TV magician Paul Daniels clearly does, and some. But in the case of some allegedly Badly Behaved guys we think everyone should <u>back off</u> and give praise where it's due.

HENRY THE VIII

There's a lot of nonsense talked these days about men who can't commit. Here was a bloke who committed... again and again. We've all been there: you find a girl, settle down in your 'palace', you think you're sorted and suddenly you bump into someone else at a do and can't get her out of your mind. All the more tricky if your current bird owns Spain. You call in your solicitor, get him to change the law, dissolve that marriage and marry your new lady. Then, would you believe it, it happens again! And again! And again. Henry had such a good solicitor that he twice managed to negotiate a divorce package that inclu-ded having his ex beheaded. We think this is simply wrong (see <u>Old Girlfriends</u>). Even so. Little known fact: in later life Henry was barred from most pubs in the Hampton Court area because he kept knocking punters' pints off the bar with his enormous belly.

ELVIS

Another king. Harried into an early grave by endless criticisms that he just dossed around all day eating junk food. If he'd been left alone to enjoy his family barrel of chicken wings washed down with a crate of Dr Pepper he might still be alive to sing to us. Little know fact: Elvis never came to this country because he thought British ice-cream tasted all watery and came in only a limited range of flavours.

RICHARD NIXON

Bugging and swearing. Not skills you automatically associate with being Head Bloke in the Western World but Dickie found time to do them both. Good man! The phrase 'expletive deleted' appears so often on the Watergate tapes he must have got through more cursing than a Leeds United supporter with Tourette's Syndrome. History does not record whether the missing words were your standard fuck shit bollocks or whether Tricky experimented with expletives like "winky-wanky-woo" and "eat scrotum, Kissinger!" Well known fact: also a brilliant liar.

GHENGIS KHAN

Founder of the Mongol empire and the original lad with energy to burn. It seems to us that his biggest crime is simply that he liked to get out and about. Ghenghis Khan means Emperor of All - a title he adopted when feeling particularly cocky after a night out with some mates. His original name was Steve Noggs. Little known fact: even when out and about rampaging across Siberia, he still found the time to co-own a nightclub called "Three Steppes To Heaven" back in Constantinople as it was then called.

KEITH MOON

There's a lot of nonsense talked about what constitutes Bad Behaviour. Much of it in this book. But let's face it, any way you look at it, Keith Moon conducted himself like a complete crazy-arse. When he died it was a black-pants day for companies that specialise in refitting hotel rooms and removing cars from swimming pools. In his memory, every year we have a Keith Moon Day when we shout a lot. Little known fact: Keith threatened to emulate Frank Zappa and call his child Moon-unit, which would have made it Moon-unit Moon.

COUNTRYSIDE

It's easier to Behave Badly in towns. In the countryside, as in space, there is often nobody there to hear you scream, let alone form a crowd and listen to your repertoire of blue knock-knock jokes. We suppose it's somewhere to go for a day out with your new special lady, bless her, although you'll end up feeling obliged to have sex in a field, wasps will descend on you and she will start screaming and weeping until you are forced to pull out, leaving you angry and frustrated.

CRAZY HORSES'

A song to be sung when you are so drunk it almost scares you. Got the Osmonds the number 2 spot in the charts in 1972, its rightful place at number 1 was denied ironically by Little Jimmy Osmond's Long Haired Lover From Liverpool for which may he burn in Pop Hell for all eternity. An anthem to Bad Behaviour, Crazy Horses has the greatest chorus of all time. Start by intoning the words 'crazy horses' in an artificially low voice, then launch your voice upwards in a weird, piercing whelp and shout "Wah! Wah!" Do this three or four dozen times. Don't worry about the other words - nobody knows them apart from the current curator of The Osmond Museum in Salt Lake City.

See also 'Lady In Red', 'Sailing' and 'Hi-Ho Silver Lining'.

CYNICISM

We don't agree with it. We believe we were put here to suck magic moments out of the chaos of life, be it by drinking lager till we get 'the burn' or by paying physical homage to girls. But we do believe in being cynical about the following: Hoovering, Parents, Bitter-drinkers, Herbs and Spices. All politicians except Kenneth Clark. Doctors with goatee beards. Snooker player Cliff Thorburn.

CHUCKING GIRLS

Nobody says this is easy. In fact, us Blokes often find it so hard to blow the final whistle on a relationship that we never actually do it and end up spending the rest of our lives with someone we only got off with because they were standing in front of the door to the Men's kharzi.

The reason for our squeamishness is nothing to do with cowardice and everything to do with us all being gentle, sensitive souls who can't bear to inflict pain or hurt on someone we love and respect.OK. It's ALL to do with cowardice.

Here then are a few pointers to help you, Bill McClaren would say, Do The Needful.

Reasons to Give
a)   "I've just found out I'm sterile and it's just not fair to you to carry on"
     (A couple of farewell shags to follow and you're home and dry)
b)   "I'm sorry but I just have a biological need to shag other women"
     (Brilliant. You're not chucking her as such just making it impossible for her to keep going out with you)
c)   "My therapist says I need space to grow as a person"
     (Wonderful on Mandies who automatically equate Therapy with lunacy)
d)   "I don't love you and I probably never have"
     (Brutal but 100% effective. Unlikely to end in a farewell shag)

Reasons Not to Give
a)   "I think I love you too much"
     (To a woman you can never love them too much)
b)   "Well, let's face it, you're not exactly Kylie, are you?"
     (Cue long argument about what's so great about Kylie)
c)   "I've decided you're genetically unsuitable to bear my children"
     (She'll think you're broody and fight all the harder to hold onto you)
d)   "I think I'm gay"
     (All too plausible. Besides you know how rumours spread)

Places to Do It
a)   Busy street, while the sales are on
b)   Departure lounge, just before you fly out for 6 month trip to Australia
c)   At the altar - it'll be just like that brilliant bit in Four Weddings...
d)   Via office E-mail. All her friends will know and come to comfort her

Places Not To Do It
a)   Her car, while she's driving
b)   The same place where you met her
c)   Her bed, while you're knobbing her best friend
d)   Via the scoreboard at Wembley - she'll never see it

For further advice on dealing with your Ex see OLD GIRLFRIENDS

CHUCKING UP

BLURRGH

The desire or need to chuck up has long been a source of shame in our culture. This is curious as along with such things as eating, sleeping and watching kids programmes on a Saturday it's something that all of us do.

Mind you, not all of us get it right all of the time so if you want to avoid the disgrace of parking your pavement pizza in the wrong place (ie, not on the pavement) then why not follow these few simple rules...

1. Listen to what your body's telling you. If you're seeing double, your brain is swirling and your stomach is going into convulsions then maybe, JUST MAYBE that last bite of scrumpy snake-bite might not be such a good idea after all and you should get up off the floor and sort yourself out in the bogs like a man.

2. Don't listen to your friends. They want you to get so off your face that you have to throw up as this invariably means you're
a) instantly removed from whatever sexual equations are being spun that night
b) much easier to kick around the car-park like an old sack of washing.

This rule does NOT apply if what your friends are telling you is not to chuck up on the bouncer.

3. As a general rule try to avoid hurling at home-as violent Irish sports involving long wooden sticks can do untold damage to your soft furnishings. As far as actual puking goes, it may not always be possible to make it to the great white telephone (though why you'd want to phone anybody then is a deep mystery in itself) in which case you could settle for these simple alternatives:
a) Your flatmates guitar. Not only does it hold gallons of the stuff but it'll also stop him playing 'Here comes the Sun' for a week or two.
b) A Yucca Plant. Yuccas hate vomit and it's as good a way of killing the bastards off as any known to man

Places where it's NOT a good idea to chuck onto/into include:
a) Your bed
b) Your kettle
c) Your pet
d) Your girlfriend's brand new trainers

COCKTAILS

The Hippy Shake

3 measures of unfiltered scrumpy
1 measure river water
2 measures dandelion tea
1 pint of homemade real ale
Sprinkle with eviction notices
and serve in a damp teepee
with 18 minutes of American
Indian drum solos

The White Stiletto

1 measure Advocat
1 measure Baileys
2 measures Taboo, Mirage
and creme de menthe frappé
Half pint cheap frascati wine
Top up with diet lemonade
Serve with glacé cherry and
Kevin Costner video

The Estate Agent

1 Bottle Ice Lager
5 measures of healthy scepticism
Sprinkle with itching powder and
serve under wheels of speeding
truck

The Luvvie

Half pint warm champagne
3 measures vodka and tonic
1 measure sacharine
2 measures bitter
1 Measure for Measure
Garnish liberally with heaps
of insincere praise and serve
with closure notice

The Biker

1 mug of warm tea
Half can of Special Brew (sod it,
bung the whole lot in)
1 gallon Castrol GTX
Serve with oily rag and hours of
tedious conversation
about gear ratios

'Er Indoors

1 measure cooking sherry
2 measures ameretto baking liquer
Pint of skimmed milk
Pour onto a bed of crushed Prozac.
Serve with a pile of ironing and
a signed photo of Richard and Judy

The Minister

16 measures frozen vodka
1 measure clear blue water
3 measures designed to push back
the frontiers of the state
Garnish with crushed lives
and broken promises
Serve on board of privatised
utility

CLARE GROGAN

Some bright stars are destined to burn but for a short time and sadly Clare's has long since felt the irresistible pull of gravity and collapsed into a Black Hole. Quite how this happened is a mystery as deep as the laws of physics themselves for few ladies have held sway over the nation's trousers like our Clare did in the early 80's. Grown men have been known to weep at the very thought of her appearance on Top Of The Pops with Altered Images, dancing around like a manic doll with an usually large sexual appetite. To our knowledge there are at least two people who share the same fantasy that one day Clare will burst out of the cake in her Loopy Loo blue rah-rah skirt and give them a very Happy Birthday indeed. Meantime, it's back to the pause button and the Gregory's Girl video. Let's hope the selfish bastard Glaswegians who've been keeping her to themselves all these years drown in luke-warm porridge.

CENTAUR

A creature out of Greek legend that was half bloke, half horse. Not much point in that arrangement, surely, although quite nice for the ladies. Here are some hybrids we'd like to see in Britain, ideally by the year 2000:

Kymate. Half-Kylie, half-mate. It is happy to spend all evening at the bar with you talking about how its new Ford Mondeo is handling, but when you get home it turns into an Antipodean temptress with the voice of an angel. Suddenly you only need one person in your life.

Mermaid. Half-Paul Merton, half-barmaid. Offers similar value to the Kymate, except this creature has the large welcoming breasts, easy manner and full range of lagers of a barmaid, combined with the wit of South London's drollest comedian.

Spannerman. Half-man, half-toolbox. Its head and torso is human, its lower body is a sturdy metal casing with various compartments containing spanners and suchlike. So when you're working on your gearbox at the weekend, get Spannerman over, keep him talking and meanwhile make shameless use of his tools.

Pitapin. Half-pitbull terrier, half-terrapin. The ideal pet, because unusual enough to get you chatting to girls at the busstop.

CONTRACEPTION

They say there's no such thing as a free lunch and the possibility that a bit of harmless fun can lead to a lifetime of nappies is the bill hanging over each and every time you get a free shot on goal in the six yard box.

With that in mind it's as well to be as wised up on the various life-saving options as you can be without sounding like a student doctor.

THE PILL: Undoubtedly the greatest invention of the 20th century, if not in the entire history of the world. Grown men have been known to weep at the simple beauty of the idea that, thanks to a simple white ball of solidified chemicals, they can leap on a complete stranger and spread their seed with the gay abandon of a pissed-up Idaho wheat Farmer. Sadly, the Pill's status as one of the shock troops of the Sexual Revolution has been buggered up by various medical nasties and happy is the man indeed who finds a girl who keeps a little silver packet of chemicals by her bedside. If you do, then you should probably ask her to marry you on the spot.

THE CONDOM: The Nigel Mansells of the contraceptive world; dull, awkward, and as spontaneous as a joke at the Tory party conference. Try to pack as exotic a range of styles, colours and flavours as possible, though you should only use Mint if you find yourself with a Prossie in a car-park in L.A.

THE CAP - the second best alternative to the Pill as it doesn't take any spin off your ball and it's up to the chick in question to sort it out. Watch out for bruises on your helmet though when you try anything past page 47 of the Karma Sutra for Dummies.

COITUS INTERRUPTUS - you WHAT? Only an institution as full of old farts and child abusers as the Catholic Church could even think about this as a viable option. Horizontal jogging should only be interrupted for three things - a fag, a swig of lager and for stammering your excuse when your girlfriend comes home early from her holidays.

Alternative Uses For Contraception

WEE, LOOK, MUMMY!

KIDS CASTLE

PIIL - bird seed, breath freshener, poker chips, powering bath-time model submarine

FEMIDON - bin liner, bouncy castle for kids, weapon for Gladiator style fighting games

CONDOM - freezer bags for small carrots, money pouch, for rest see JONNI-GARMI

CAP - micro herb garden, baby's frisbee, bird bath, fake flying saucer

bend up + down

ncy aerial for receiving h Special on Radio 4

Emergency Contraception

In the heat of the moment you might be tempted to think that almost anything will do. Sadly this is just not the case.

BUBBLE GUM - too sticky, gets caught in her hair, hard to get rid of afterwards

CLING FILM - builds up static, can be sweaty and often gets tangled in your hands. Keeps your lunchbox fresh and, if scare-stories are right, plays merry hell with your sperm count.

BIN LINER - see FEMIDOM above

SELLOTAPE - doesn't work, hurts like hell when you pull it off, and you can spend hours of valuable love time trying to find the beginning of the roll

RUBBER GLOVE - generally a bad idea as it reminds girlies of their last trip to their gynaecologist

DIRTY MAGS, Shopping for

SEEDY MAN BEHIND COUNTER

Pornography demeans women... Pornography arrests men's emotional development... Pornography distorts interpersonal relationships... Whether or not you think that that nonsense is true, somehow you have to get hold of the stuff.

Current data indicates that 93% of males in this country between the ages of 18 and 50 maintain a collection of pornographic magazines in the home. Some keep them at the back of their jumper drawer, some dip them in a special fluid which disguises them as the June issue of the magazine Practical Boat Owner, some leave them at their friend Keith's house. The mags range from homely publications like Mayfair, (the porn equivalent of a mug of cocoa) to hard-core grubbiness like ArschEkstase (the porn equivalent of six pints of plutonium).

Where do we buy this stuff? Down at the local newsagents. How do we buy it? With all the subtlety and precision of the raid on Entebbe in 1976 to free the Israeli hostages, only using fewer firearms obviously.

1. Ascertain location of target material through smeary glass of newsagents' window. Check that you didn't go to school with the shop assistant.

UNSUSPECTING SHOPKEEPER

COUNTER

SWEETS | CARDS | FILTH

YOU →

SWEATY

2. Enter shop, moving in opposite direction to magazine section. Pick up 'Congratulations you Have Learnt to Swim' card. Study with more fascination than if it held the secret of life itself. Wait for old man to finish buying chewing-tobacco. Put down card. Pick up 'Sorry You Crashed Your Lawnmower' card.

3. Let eyes drift over to top shelf of magazines. Make mental selection.

4. Move over to periodicals sections. Wait for two small children to spend thirteen minutes buying a Dime bar. Scan the premises for relatives, neighbours, friends, anyone who's ever known you, and your girlfriend (if any).

5. Make rapid selection and approach counter. Purchase, avoiding all eye contact. Feel sordid and ridiculous but strangely excited.

CENSORED

Dancing

Never, _ever_ dance when you're sober. That's the only rule. And never watch yourself dancing on home videos. If you do you'll never want to 'get off the wall' again. Those are the only two rules. Dancing is self-expression, it's the body tuning in to its own rhythms, it's a primitive war-jig, it's a blah blah blah blah. Here are the major Bad Behaviour styles.

The Solo. Dancing, they say, is like having sex, only standing up. If that is true there's an awful lot of masturbation going on up and down the country. Step one: arrange your greasy hair so that it falls across your face. Step two: stand near the speaker. Step three: whirl around like a 10p piece on the spin cycle with no regard to the safety of other dancers (if any) or the music.

The Dirty Dance. This still works best with Three Times A Lady, the only song in the history of pop which has a direct radio link with a lady's lady's area. Start with some vague actual dancing then gradually clutch your totty to you. Within thirty seconds your groins should be fused more tightly than a piece of high-class German welding. Spend the last couple of minutes of the song apologising huskily for your erection.

Flash Dance. We've all seen Come Dancing. Some of us have even done it (see above). It's ugly and ridiculous. Still, flash slick dancing does seem to impress the girls, bless 'em. Here's how you do it. 1. Slap on a litre tub of fake tan. 2. Squeeze into a girl's blouse and shell suit slacks. 3. Strut around, smiling as though you're having a heart attack but are determined to finish the dance. 4. Do lots of pointless sharp movements of your head as though someone's just shouted "Wanker!" at you across the dancefloor and you want to find out who it was.

The About-To-Collapse Shuffle. Also known as The Last Dance. To be carried out with a fag in one hand, lager can in the other. Words are to be sung along to the music, even if it's an instrumental.

DRUGS

As we all know drugs are dangerous things, not just for the harm they do to your body but the incredible damage they do to your fashion sense. If this weren't reason enough not to touch drugs here's a few other things that can happen if you stray beyond the bounds of the law:

LSD
Who wants to take something that sounds like an exam board? This is for beardies in Somerset only.

Ecstasy
Makes you want to run about too much and drink orange juice. Anything that affects the appetite for lager must be avoided.

Heroine
You've got to be a member of the aristocracy and been buggered at school for ten years before you can go near it. Anyway, anything involving that many needles can't be much fun.

Marijuana
Behaving badly depends on shouting - when you've smoked too much dope, you can't even speak, let alone shout. However, if you're chatting up an art-school bird, it is vital to say that you've smoked dope, but that it didn't do anything for you. This way you can sound cool, while at the same time saving yourself the embarrassment of smoking dope for the first time later in the evening back at her place and ending up puking all over her genuine Arabian birthing rug.

Cocaine
You've got to change your name to Tarquin, get a job in the city, wear red braces and be a terminal wanker before you can take this. Much easier to just go down the offy and get a six-pack.

Basically, life is our drug... Apart from caffeine, nicotine, alcohol and staying up late watching programmes on the Open University. And what's dangerous about that?

Speed
Great film starring Sandra Bullock. Shame she had to spoil it all by snogging Kenau Reeves at the end.

DANGEROUS SPORTS

The main purpose of Dangerous Sports is to introduce a note of peril and excitement into otherwise dull lives which is precisely why they offer so little to the Badly Behaved bloke that he can't get by sleeping with his mate's girlfriend (again) or walking across the sofa with a full pint of lager balanced on his head.

Still marketing managers have to do something at the weekends and if your idea of fun is dressing up in anoraks and throwing yourself off or down or through things you were never meant to then all we can say is please DO NOT:

a) Accompany your act by shouting "Yowser" or whooping a lot and saying 'Alright' in what you fondly imagine to be a cool Californian accent. Remember you are not an American teenager but an ordinary British bloke who lives in Baldock and drives a basic company Vauxhall.
b) Think for one second that by staring death in the face at an adventure centre in North Wales that you've suddenly become a better or more interesting person. You haven't. You've just got very wet and got the piss taken out of you by the beardies who really know how to do it.
c) Come round here looking for sympathy when you fall over and hurt yourself.

Rather than lay out good money for some so called 'expert' to organise your dangerous sports why not try these cheap and even more thrilling alternatives in the comfort of your own home.

a) Budgie Jumping: forget lengths of elastic and tedious equations involving height and weight. All you have to do is take one budgie and jump over it(admittedly this is probably only dangerous to the budgie.)

b) White Water Rafting: It's amazing what you can achieve with a teatray, a hose-pipe, a family size packet of Persil and someone else's stairs.

dREAMS, INTERPRETATIONS OF

A lot of rubbish has been written about dreams and what they might be really about. This is especially true of Bloke's Dreams which people like Freud say are mostly about our deep psychic need to sleep with our mothers and mangle our dad's landing gear in the lawn mower. What a load of bollocks. Have you seen most people's mothers? Maybe this Freud bloke should just stick to flogging dog food on the tele and trying to remember the names of all his famous daughters instead.

This is the definitive guide to what those weird dreams really mean. And we should know. We've had all of them.

YOU'RE FALLING OFF A HIGH BUILDING
You're scared of heights or you forgot to put the protective rails up on your bed.

YOU'RE PILOTING THE GRAFF ZEPPELIN
Now who's a lucky boy then?

YOU'RE LOST IN A DENSE FOREST
This is a sex dream. The forest is an adorable woman's pubic hair. You are, well, you. You like giving oral sex which is why you're happy to wander around for hours. If you didn't you would simply use the compass in the heel of your Clarke's Attackers to navigate your way out again.

YOU WANT TO GET AWAY FROM SOMETHING BUT YOU CAN'T MOVE YOUR LEGS
This is a girlfriend dream. Is she tying you down too much? Can you really be free in a long running relationship? Is seeing her once a month proving a little too much for you?

YOU'RE TAKING A PENALTY IN THE WORLD CUP FINAL AND YOU MISS
This is what Terry Venables would call a training opportunity. Look carefully at your technique, analyse the faults in your run up, your address of the ball etc. and put it right next time.

YOU'RE MARRIED TO JANET JACKSON
Your brain is planning for the future and looking on the bright side. Saying yes to Janet when she pops the question is just another option for a young, attractive man at the height of his sexual powers.

YOU'RE MARRIED TO MICHAEL JACKSON
Now this is an interesting one. Ask yourself. Were you ever a boy scout, an altar boy or a border at an isolated minor public school? If the answer's yes then this is probably less of a dream and more of a recovered memory.

YOU'RE SHAGGING YOUR SISTER
No one ever has this dream. Not ever. No.

ALRIGHT CLAUDIA, IF YOU MUST.

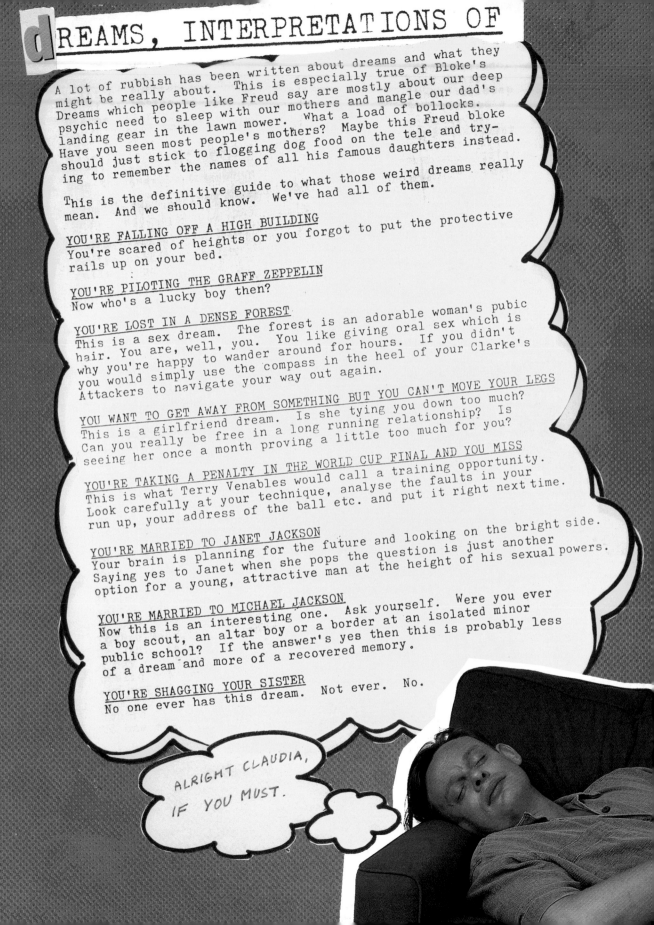

In these days of grunting butch baseliners tennis is not the spectator sport it once was. This has nothing to do with the actual quality of the play and everything to do with the sad fact that there are few, if indeed any, women players whose skirts you would wish to see flutter upwards in the gentle Wimbledon breeze. It wasn't always so, especially when our little Chrissie was donning her pink-laced pumps and blowing more crusty old dykes away than a Nazi panzer division raging through Holland.

Chrissie had style, Chrissie had grace Chrissie had perfect skin and ponytails. Everything she did was femininity itself - from the way she blew stray hairs out of her eyes to the delightfully adolescent bite she gave her top lip while she was crouched down waiting to return serve. Most importantly of all Chrissie had a great sense of drama and took us to the edge match after match with the same heart-stopping question - would they be frilly or would they be plain? Luckily for us - and the game of tennis as a whole - there was usually only one answer.

JACULATION, PREMATURE

The obvious question, it has been pointed out, is "Excuse me - premature for who exactly?" Still, try thinking of these to delay the inevitable:

- Bruce Forsythe squatting on a glass table

- The Apollo 10 Lunar Module Airfix kit

- Your all-time top three cheeses

- Chancellor Helmut Kohl of Germany squatting on a glass table

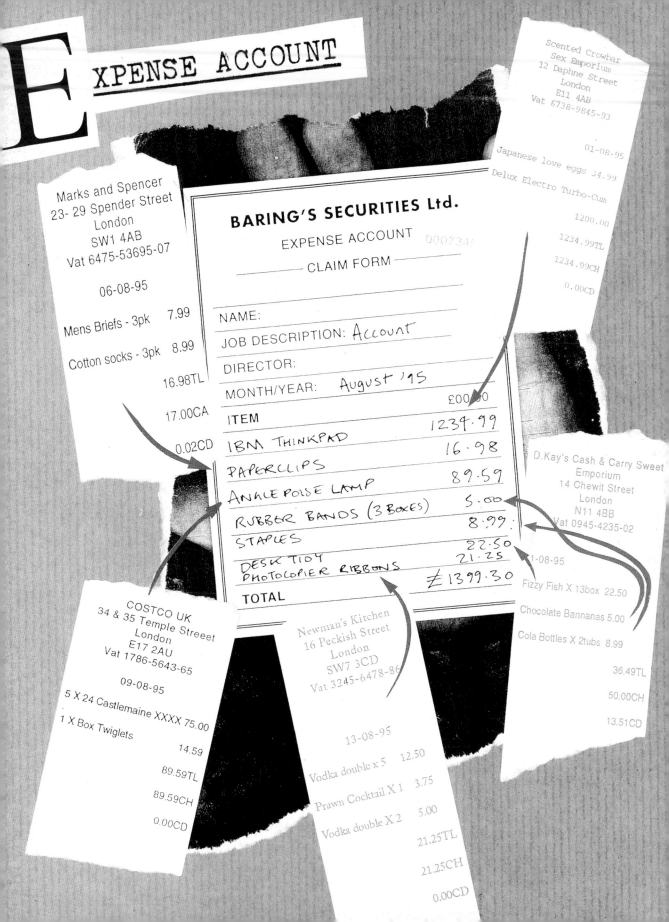

EXPENSE ACCOUNT

Marks and Spencer
23- 29 Spender Street
London
SW1 4AB
Vat 6475-53695-07

06-08-95

Mens Briefs - 3pk   7.99

Cotton socks - 3pk 8.99

16.98TL

17.00CA

0.02CD

Scented Crowbar
Sex Emporium
12 Daphne Street
London
E11 4AB
Vat 6738-9845-93

01-08-95

Japanese love eggs 34.99

Delux Electro Turbo-Cum

1200.00

1234.99TL

1234.99CH

0.00CD

BARING'S SECURITIES Ltd.

EXPENSE ACCOUNT
000734?

CLAIM FORM

NAME:

JOB DESCRIPTION: *Account*

DIRECTOR:

MONTH/YEAR: *August '95*

£00.00

ITEM	
IBM THINKPAD	1234.99
PAPERCLIPS	16.98
ANGLEPOISE LAMP	89.59
RUBBER BANDS (3 BOXES)	5.00
STAPLES	8.99
DESK TIDY	22.50
PHOTOCOPIER RIBBONS	21.25
TOTAL	≠ 1399.30

D.Kay's Cash & Carry Sweet
Emporium
14 Chewit Street
London
N11 4BB
Vat 0945-4235-02

1-08-95

Fizzy Fish X 13box 22.50

Chocolate Bannanas 5.00

Cola Bottles X 2tubs 8.99

36.49TL

50.00CH

13.51CD

COSTCO UK
34 & 35 Temple Streeet
London
E17 2AU
Vat 1786-5643-65

09-08-95

5 X 24 Castlemaine XXXX 75.00

1 X Box Twiglets

14.59

89.59TL

89.59CH

0.00CD

Newman's Kitchen
16 Peckish Street
London
SW7 3CD
Vat 3245-6478-86

13-08-95

Vodka double x 5   12.50

Prawn Cocktail X 1 3.75

Vodka double X 2   5.00

21.25TL

21.25CH

0.00CD

f LYING

Unlike women us blokes have no fear of flying. After all-most of us spend pretty much our whole life doing it, admittedly by the seat of our pants. To blokes trips on planes are the ultimate treat, offering unparalleled opportunities to Behave very Badly indeed in a confined space that, by some strange quirk, exists outside the bounds of social norms and national law. A few special points though spring to mind.

1. **Air Hostesses**— Don't even think about it. Hostesses are only ever pulled in mid-seventies movies. What's more if you think she looks bored during the safety lecture imagine how you'd feel if she pulled the same face during sex. Much better to concentrate instead on...

2. **The Girl Sitting Beside You** - now we're talking. This is much more promising territory because;

a) She's strapped in beside you for the rest of the flight.
b) The drinks are free so you can afford to be generous.
c) She knows nothing about you and you are totally at liberty to re-invent yourself as the social sexual success you would dearly like to be in real life.
d) You have endless shared topics of conversation - airplane food, the other passengers, the in-flight magazine and disaster stories. If these come up, why not stare out at the wing, look worried for a moment and, having sworn you saw the engine wobble, wait till she starts to blub loudly on your shoulder. If she's drunk enough you could be stroking her hair and kissing her ear within minutes.

3. The Mile High Club-a mythical entity whose membership is mostly made up of the sad fantasists who really do write in letters to Mayfair (plus, of course, Rod Stewart). Unfortunately, in these days of cheap seats andfull flights, it's almost impossible to even get into a loo at all never mind find time to perform erotically charged acts with complete strangers. Don't be surprised if you have to settle for the Half -Mile Club. If you need membership requirements of this spelt out you're probably reading the wrong book.

4. In-Flight Movies-forget headphones .Why not pass the time away more constructively by doing all those voices yourself? You'll find this goes down particularly well with irascible wrinklies and low rent businessmen slumming it in economy class. If all else fails pretend the person next to you is really deaf and shout out the ending.

5. Duty Frees-of course nobody with any sense actually buys duty-frees on the plane as you've already loaded up well past your allowance in the four hour delay at the airport. Still endless fun can still be had by finding the stroppiest steward and making him talk you through every single item on the trolley before telling him that you can't buy anything as you've left all your cash in your suitcase. Of course this is only funny if you __haven't__ left all your cash in your suitcase.

FAMILY TREE

Most families are a nightmare and hardly anybody's got the Rellies they deserve. This is what a real Bloke's family should look like.

SCARY GRANDMA WHO KNOWS A LOT ABOUT SEX: DORIS LESSING

SCARY GRANDAD: RUPERT MURDOCH

NICE GRANDMA WHO KNOWS NOTHING ABOUT SEX: DORA BRYAN

AMUSING GRANDAD: PETER USTINOV

AMIABLE UNCLE WITH HOPELESS SHOWBIZ ANECDOTES: DENNIS HOPPER

SEXY AUNT: SUSAN SARANDON

COOL DAD: JACK NICHOLSON

GOOD LOOKING MUM: JOANNA LUMLEY

MAD BUT FANCIABLE AUNT: DIANE KEATON

ECCENTRIC AND SEXUALLY AMBIGUOUS UNCLE: STEPHEN FRY

MAD BUT UNFANCIABLE AUNT: GERMAINE GREER

TEDIOUS UNCLE WHO KEEPS BORING ON ABOUT ENTIRELY FICTIONAL ACHIEVEMENTS: ROY HATTERSLEY

YOU

YOUNGER SISTER COURTNEY LOVE

ELDER SISTER: AMANDA DONAHOE

ELDER BROTHER: JOHN TRAVOLTA

YOUNGER BROTHER RYAN GIGGS

COUSIN: DAVID GOWER

COUSIN: CHARLOTTE COLEMAN

NEPHEW: KEANU REEVES

SPUNKY NEICE WHO'S THE SAME AGE AS YOU: JULIA SAWALHA

DISTANT COUSIN WHO REMEMBERS BIRTHDAYS: ELTON JOHN

BLACK SHEEP: OLIVER REED

COUSIN: EMMANUELLE BEART

COUSIN: JOHN BONJOVI

FRENCH KISSING

DO:
- Accompany your kissing with muttered romantic phrases like "Mm, you taste like you have truly slipped from some ambrosial fountain quite recently" or "Brilliant!"
- tap her on the shoulder and stop if you feel faint
- remember that to avoid clashing noses one of you must rotate to the right, one of you to the left. Diagrams are available on Ceefax.

DON'T
- accompany your kissing with phrases like "What's that... thing under your tongue?" or "Eat face, Babe!"
- go on kissing if you find her tonsils, epiglottis or major stretches of her gum have entered your mouth cavity
- suddenly pull your tongue out and exclaim in disgust "You bit me, you bitch!"

FOREPLAY

There's a lot of nonsense talked about foreplay. It's not very fashionable to say so, but is it necessary, actually? Is it? Or is it one of those things which, like taking two bottles into the shower, seem logical for a brief moment in history but which don't stand up to closer scrutiny. Think about it. That's all we're saying.

FIVE-A-SIDE FOOTBALL

Unfortunately, part of being a lad involves playing, as opposed to merely watching sport. This is no fun but the pain can be minimised if you:-

a) Arrive drunk.

b) Smoke during play. (Hard, but not impossible)

c) Don't run.

gAMES, TO PLAY IN PUB

Sometimes even the best conversationalists may have run out of things to say about The Real Reason We Will Never Be Caught Dead in Flares by the time the fourth pint comes round. This is where Pub Games come in, providing a chance to keep the momentum of the evening going without resorting to scrapping or telling your mate what you really think about his girlfriend.

POOL

The pub goers snooker. Whereas a frame of snooker can, in the wrong hands, last for an entire weekend, it's statistically and geometrically impossible for any frame of pool to last more than half-an-hour. Besides, pool is far better for bullshitting, not only because nobody really knows the rules but because of all the stupid made-up words you can come out with to describe the game. Take for instance, when you mis-cue a sitter and the ball stops agonisingly close to the lip of the pocket. Duff shot? Not a bit of it. You are merely laying down a Goalkeeper to give you Death Options at the Clearage Moment.

Pool Hints

Do
a) Play negatively from the very beginning, taking every available opportunity to lay snookers and play cat and mouse with the final red ball. This will not only unsettle your opponent but irritate the fuck out of the two hard-looking blokes with moustaches who are waiting to get on the table. That'll teach them for bringing their own cues and ironing their polo shirts.
b) Use phrases like 'top', 'side', 'English' and 'skills'.

Don't
a) Bring your own cue - it's only a pub and you should at least try to look like you haven't got a tiny penis
b) Ride roughshod over any 'Winner Stays on' arrangements. No game of pool, however enjoyable, is worth dying for.

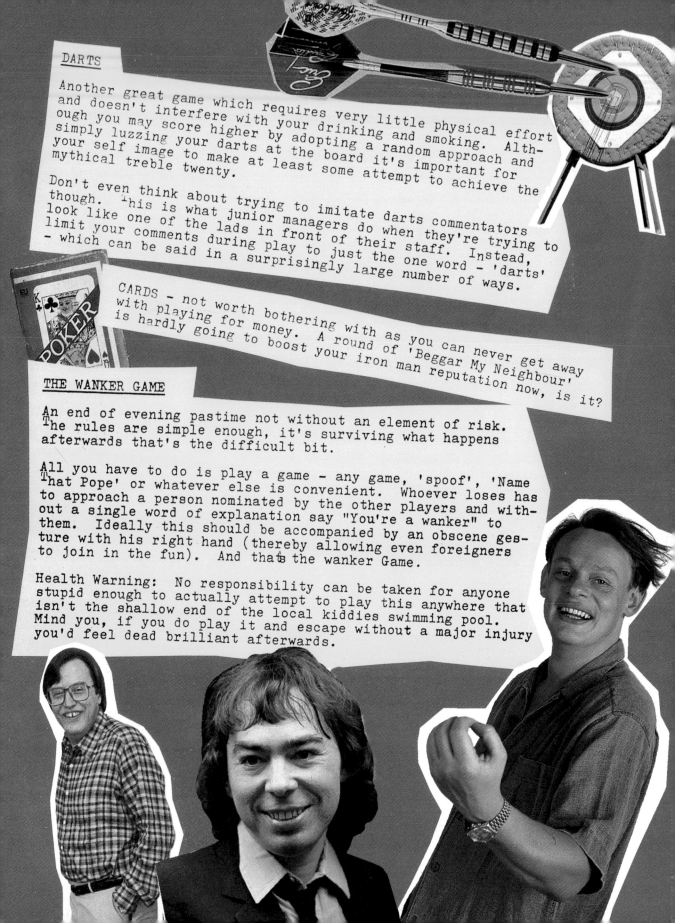

DARTS

Another great game which requires very little physical effort and doesn't interfere with your drinking and smoking. Although you may score higher by adopting a random approach and simply luzzing your darts at the board it's important for your self image to make at least some attempt to achieve the mythical treble twenty.

Don't even think about trying to imitate darts commentators though. This is what junior managers do when they're trying to look like one of the lads in front of their staff. Instead, limit your comments during play to just the one word - 'darts' - which can be said in a surprisingly large number of ways.

CARDS - not worth bothering with as you can never get away with playing for money. A round of 'Beggar My Neighbour' is hardly going to boost your iron man reputation now, is it?

THE WANKER GAME

An end of evening pastime not without an element of risk. The rules are simple enough, it's surviving what happens afterwards that's the difficult bit.

All you have to do is play a game - any game, 'spoof', 'Name That Pope' or whatever else is convenient. Whoever loses has to approach a person nominated by the other players and without a single word of explanation say "You're a wanker" to them. Ideally this should be accompanied by an obscene gesture with his right hand (thereby allowing even foreigners to join in the fun). And that's the wanker Game.

Health Warning: No responsibility can be taken for anyone stupid enough to actually attempt to play this anywhere that isn't the shallow end of the local kiddies swimming pool. Mind you, if you do play it and escape without a major injury you'd feel dead brilliant afterwards.

GOVERNMENT AND POLITICS

If you want to Behave Badly there can be few fields as promi-sing as Politics. After all in what other job do you get to swan around at tax-payers expense making a complete prat of yourself at cocktail parties and still go home with the best looking chic in the room? Just think of the perks of the MP's job.

- Researchers - remember power is the ultimate aphrodisiac and even the iciest maiden melts when confronted with a comfortable majority and a free lift in the ministerial Jag. Take full advantage by stuffing your front office with horny young Oxbridge grads with an Authority Complex.

- Speeches - make them as dull and long-winded as possible until you slip in the word 'Bollocks' just as everyone's falling asleep. This will make you hugely popular with everyone in the country and you can earn a small fortune appearing on TV as the latest Good Bloke MP. Failing that you could always dress up in a Chelsea strip and knob a failed actress.

- Party Conferences - the ultimate holiday camp complete with sun, sand and lots of silly pretending games called policy debates, at which you'll pretend that Britain Is Being Over-Run By Unmarried Lesbian Mothers and everybody else will pre-tend to agree with you.

- Sex - the availability of bouncing-botty action very much depends which party you've joined:

Tories tend to be plump, jolly and bossy. Bring a riding crop and a copy of Mein Kampf and you generally won't go far wrong.

Liberal Democrats do a nice line in recently divorced thirt something though Lib-Dems being habitual fence-sitters you'll be hard put to get them to make up their mind whethe sleep with you or not.

Labour chics are hard work though they can be rewarding if staying up late drinking mint tea and arguing about the Chilean constitution is your idea of smutty talk. Apparently if you can break through the feminist rhetoric and all that nonsense about calling each other comrade, labour ladies go like a runaway train.

Of course the real fun in politics starts when you pull the ultimate fast one and get yourself elected to run the count Unfortunately none of the parties seem likely to take full advantage of this, being stuck with the same faces and the same tired ideas about the NHS and schools. What's needed a new broom, a new set of ideas, a cabinet of new faces. Here's just a few of the changes we would make if we got t call from a desperate nation.

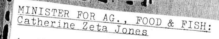

OUR CABINET

MINISTER FOR AG., FOOD & FISH:
Catherine Zeta Jones

1. All lands will be requisitioned for the widespread cultivation of hops and barley.

2. Sheep and cows to be abolished in Wales in the interests of sexual hygiene.

3. All Linda McCartney veggy-products to be burnt on a bloody great bonfire

MINISTER FOR THE TREASURY:
Carol Vorderman

1. All taxes on lager to be abolished, but doubled on Real Ale beardy-wierdys (come to think of it, beards can be taxed as well)

2. Ciggie tax to be abolished. The deficit can be made up with a net tax on Health foods and 'two-in-one' shampoos.

3. Stockbrokers and City Traders will be forced to live in rabbit hutches on Canary Wharf. Any caught in the real world will be shot on sight.

MINISTER FOR CRIME AND PUNISHMENT:
Julia Sawalha

1. Drinking coffee in pubs made a criminal offence.

2. All Estate Agents to be rounded up like sheep and made to work at sewage plants in Sheffield

3. Judges to be made to pass test on music, TV shows and useful 20th century gadgets. Failure to list top 20 on demand will be punished by having to wear wigs that make them look even more daft than they do already (eg Terry Wogan's)

MINISTER FOR TELLY: Gaby Roslin

1. Local news to be abolished and replaced with rap videos -preferably ones filmed on an especially hot day in California.

2. Sex and Bad Language to be monitored closely. Indecently hasty sex-scenes and use of repla-cement words like 'frigging' to be banned as an offence to public taste

MINISTER FOR CULTURE:
Sam from EastEnders

1. Actors to be forbidden to describe being paid to snog actresses as 'work'.

2. 'Take That' will be exiled to Baghdad, along with Boyzone, East 17 and anyone else who gives the ladies the wrong idea about how fit men should be.

3. All fat slappers in Operas to be replaced by fit chics like Whitney Huston, Sade, 'Five Star' and Whig-field.

MINISTER FOR HEALTH: Eric Bristow

1. Blue Balls sufferers to be made a national priority. Guidelines are:
a/After 2 months of sexual drought, a patient can claim a free 'massage'
b/After 4 months, he's entitled to a half-hour session with a quali-fied consultant kisser
c/After 6 months, it's the full treatment. In the interests of fairness all extras will be paid for by the patient. Obviously this doesn't include rubberwear.

2. Winging Wrinklies to be banned from time-wasting 'chats' with local G.Ps. Instead they will be made to do something useful like doing the shopping for busy working people.

OLIDAYS

Like anything that involves a lot of time, money and trips to Boots, Blokes' Holidays are poised on the thinnest knife edge between triumph and disaster. All those plans, all those hopes and expectations, all those tragic nights sitting in grotty Spanish bars staring at your mate wondering where all the women have gone. More often than not you come back broke, burnt and in such a frenzy of sexual frustration that it can take months to recover. Still all work and no play makes Jack very unlikely to be romping in the surf with a Danish Junior marketing executive and if you wanna have fun you're gonna have to head for the sun somtime. It's just a question of going about it in the right way.

CHOOSING YOUR HOLIDAY

This is the hard part. After all, how do you really <u>know</u> if Kos is a sophisticated yet youthful holiday venue or just another place where professional mothers with voices like amplified fog-horns throw quite unnecessary wobblies at their kids? The answer, of course, is research.

<u>Brochures</u>: though second only to the underwear section of the Next Direct catalogue as winter bedtime reading, brochures are no use at all for actually choosing a holiday as only girls and train-spotters can be bothered to decipher all those symbols and work their way through the price charts.

<u>Your Mates</u>: by far the most reliable source of information, not least of all because some of them will have actually visited the places they're discoursing learnedly about. When soliciting opinions, take a pad and a pencil, diligently write down every single recommendation/prejudice and then instantly book yourself in the one place they all swear blind nobody but nobody in their right mind would ever want to go to. This will almost certainly be the place with the clean beaches, elegant art deco hotels and young Italian waitresses in ridiculously short tops.

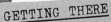

GETTING THERE

However tempting other modes of transport may seem flying is the one way to go on holiday. It's clean, it's quick, it's clinical and it's much less stressful that charging down a crowded autovia arguing with your mate about who's going to fork out 9 million pesetas for the next motorway toll. Besides which 48 hour delays at the airport, four hours of turbulence and a lukewarm airline mutton stew are a vital part of the Great British Holiday experience.

THE HOTEL

Try not to have unrealistic expectations of your lodgings and you'll rarely be disappointed. Remember unless you're a scouser signing on in Bournemouth, hotels are not your home and don't need to be palaces for you to have a good time. In fact, generally the worse they are the better as proper five star gaffs are unlikely to take kindly to you using your mattress as a makeshift lilo and signing all your bar bills over to 'the fat kraut in the hawaiian shirt'. Instead use your hotel as a launch pad for the real purpose of the Holiday...

HOLIDAY ROMANCES

These divide into two broad categories - British Birds and Foreign Birds. In both the object is very much the same - getting as much smutty, meaningless sex as you can with people whose names you can barely pronounce.

a)   British birds

Be careful. Though it may look easy enough - no boyfriends, huge Bacardi and cokes, see through tee-shirts and euro-hits - some British birds have this weird idea that their holiday romance should be, well, Romantic. Cue endless hand-holding long walks on the beach and a slow lingering seduction process that can severely eat into your available boffing time. Much better to go for the jugular straight away - trains and tunnels on the beach within the first half hour or forget it. This is particularly effective with ladies from the Greater Manchester area.

b)   Foreign Birds

The thing about Foreign birds is that by the time you roll up to them like a big grinning puppy they've heard every possible line a million times before. If you want to get anywhere you have to try something really original, really wild. You have to say something to them in their own language. It's a Rule of Life that everybody loves to hear a cute foreigner talking to them in a ridiculous accent and before you know it you'll be back in at your hotel listening to her speaking English and conjugating all kinds of verbs ending in ING. Of course you've got to have something to actually say to them to start the ball rolling. Don't be bland. Go for it by using a great line of local literature or poetry that's incredibly famous in their country and completely unknown elsewhere. As well as stopping them in their tracks it makes you seem cultured, poetic, sensitive. After all, look what a few rhymes did for Lord Byron in Italy - and he was a sickly ponce with dodgy hair and a club foot.

All of the following are especially effective if said with a choke in the voice, staring out to sea at dusk.

(FRANCE)
'Mon enfant, ma soeur,
Songe a la douceur
D'aller la-bas vivre ensemble'
"My child, my sister, imagine the sweet joy of going over there to live together"

This is by the 19th century poet Baudelaire who wrote verse of such erotic power that thousands of French girlies felt utterly compelled to sleep with him. Of course, being French, nobody takes the living together bit at all seriously.

(SPAIN)
'Que es la vida? La vida es sueno'
What is life? Life is a dream

This by the Spanish playwright Calderon and is their equivalent of "To be or not to be". The speech goes on for ages and you should cunningly suggest that you know the rest but are too weighed down by its profundity to quote it.

(ITALY)
'L'amor che move il sole e l'altre stelle'
Love that moves the sun and other stars

This is by Dante. It isn't much cop on a cloudy day.

(GERMANY)
'Lass uns chaotisch sein'-
Let us be chaotic together

This is the German revolutionary poet Eric Muhsam. To a German the idea of being Chaotic is bewilderingly daring and sexy, especially if you can be Chaotic in a clean tidy way out of sight of their parents.

THE BEACH

The beach is the battle-ground upon which the success of your holiday lives or dies. If you allow yourself to come over all shy and British and spend the whole time lying on your front desperately eye-balling every woman in sight but never talking to any of them you'll probably end your holiday in a white coat at the local looney-bin. Be kind to yourself. Get in there, give it a bash and see what happens.

Of course the best way to do this is never to bring a lighter onto the beach as asking chics for 'feu, 'Feuer' and fuego' are sure-fire ways of getting that first conversational run on the board. Non-smokers have to rely on other tricks, the best of which is the old 'Do You Know What This Word Means' manoeuvre with the local paper. If the bird's a foreigner she will try to tell you in delightfully broken English and off off you go. If she's British she won't have a clue and off you go again. NB This doesn't work if, quite by chance, the word you have selected has sexual connotations and/or refers to the rise of Neo-Nazism.

A FEW OTHER POINTS

TOUR GUIDES

Not worth bothering with as they all have beefy local boy-friends who run the wind-surfing concession on the beach. Still, it's great fun watching other people try and you can cause all kinds of mischief by telling any estate agents or computer programmers that your Guide has a crush on them.

PHOTOS

What's the point? Even if you don't lose your camera or don't forget to load the film you'll only end up with hundreds of pictures of your mate's bum on the balcony. Besides, photo labs are such moralistic bastards now that any pictures worth taking will only be immediately forwarded to the Police.

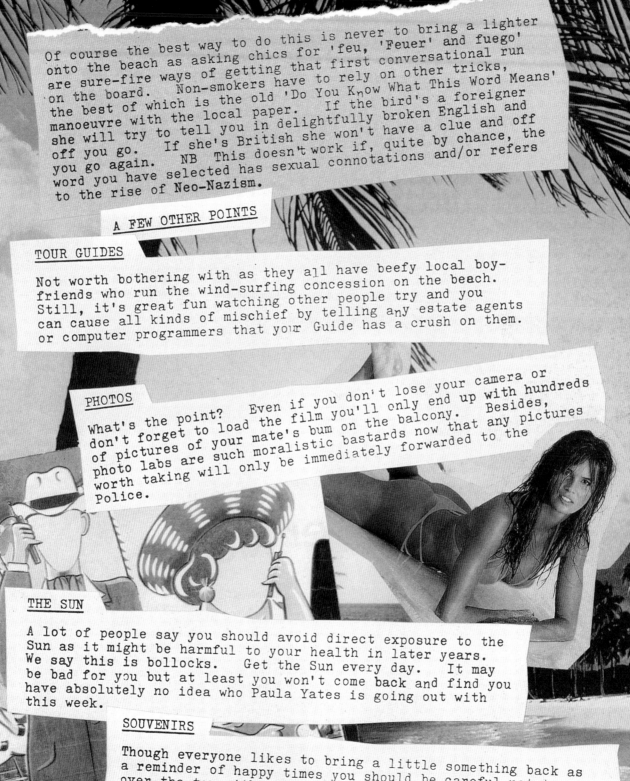

THE SUN

A lot of people say you should avoid direct exposure to the Sun as it might be harmful to your health in later years. We say this is bollocks. Get the Sun every day. It may be bad for you but at least you won't come back and find you have absolutely no idea who Paula Yates is going out with this week.

SOUVENIRS

Though everyone likes to bring a little something back as a reminder of happy times you should be careful not to go over the top with your acquisitions. Though nicking a fourteen foot Doric column from the Pantheon may have seemed like a real achievement at the time it's likely to cost you an arm and a leg in excess baggage. Likewise be very wary about trying to bring local flora and fauna back with you. Greek dogs are especially dodgy, unless she's prepared to pay her own air-fare.

HAIRCUTS

When you hit eighteen you no longer want a wheezy middle-aged barber circling your head with a spitty roll-up in his gob. You want your hair cut by a girl. It's a comfort to know that, even if you haven't had sex since Wham! split up, once a month a coiffeuse's breasts will hover a few inches from your ear and her hips will press against you as you sit under your black shroud thing looking like a Walnut Whip.

So why oh why oh why are salons always playing the following trick on their male punters. They fill the place with sexy girl hairdressers. You are passing the window, see that the place is tottytastic and enter in a state of whimpering excitement, Immediately, from the basement or the back room, some swarthy ponce comes out, whips his scissors out of his impossibly tight jeans and before you can say "You don't understand, I need the healing touch of a woman - breasts and hips and so on" he's telling you in a thick Mediterranean accent that he's going to feather your hair into a point, layer it, flip it over and for all you care put it in a box and set fire to it.

Have the strength of mind to brush him aside, swivel to the best-looking of his colleagues and, pointing at her like Lord Kitchener on that poster (not that he was recruiting hairdressers, quite the opposite), say "I want YOU to do my hair!" You will want to chat to her. However attractive she is, her questions might be a little on the stale side. Here are some suggested responses:

Q. Doing anything nice for the weekend?
A. Yes, rolling you in peanut oil and basting you with our love juice.

Q. Not working today?
A. No, sitting here wondering whether when you're about to have sex you say "I'll just get Janice to wash that for you."

Q. Been on holiday this year?
A. Yes, Quentin Tarrantino, Mickey Rourke, Brad Pitt and me went and ran with the bulls in Pamplona. Bruce Willis wanted to come but we wouldn't tell him where we were staying.

HAIR - MORNING HAIR

INNOVATIONS

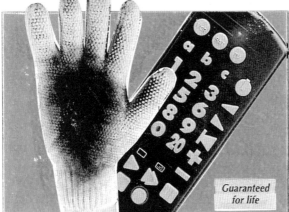

Guaranteed for life

Magic TV Gloves

Magiglove
UB 24536
£29.95

This stunning ergonomic glove is lined with special magnets to attract remote control units. Say good bye to fumbling under the sofa for the doofah, often emerging instead with a stiff old sock in your hand.

ALL free P&P

LOOK AT YOU, YOU ARSE YOU'RE DRIBBLING!

Before | After

Verbaliser
UB 26536
£19.95

Abusive Alarm Clock

At last, an alarm clock that uses language you can understand. The ten phrases become more abusive the longer you lie in: "Oy mate, how much longer are you gonna lie there?", "Time to shoot off, you lazy bastard", "Get up you utter wanker" and so on, rising to a right ticking off!

Go sick the easy way

Want to throw a sickie from work and sound convincing? Of course you do, we all do. *Skive-alive!* is the ideal solution. It distorts your voice with amazing convincingness. There are four settings: food poisoning, flu, dead relative, hit by a bus. Also comes with a scrambler to

Skive-alive!
UB 563798
£34.95

make you sound like your mother, girlfriend, passing pedestrian or local GP.

HELLO IM ILL

Tattoo Yourself in Bed

The temporary tattoo that could change your life permanently! The stunner you have admired for years refuses steadfastly to go out with you or even sleep with you. Buy the TattooMan stencil set and show her just how serious you are. Even if she hates you, now she'll feel too guilty not to share her life with you, or at least to let you jump on once!

TattooMan
UB 75836
£29.95

Aftershave Alarm

We've all heard of smoke alarms. We've heard of car alarms. But how many of us have failed to be alerted when we overdo the after-shave, in some cases causing smarting to loved-ones' eyes and even scarring their lungs. It could mean the difference between keeping your girl and losing her to another guy. Emits an amusing high-pitched squeal.

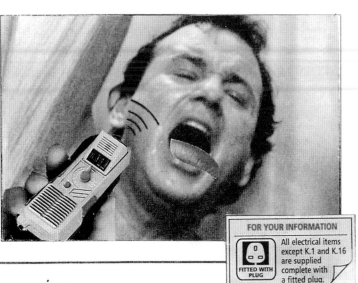

AftershaveAlarm

UB 6437458

£39.95

Drinking Companion

Drinking alone is never as much fun as drinking with a like-spirited mate. But mates are sometimes busy doing other things. Avoid looking like Norman NoFriends by purchasing Travis. Prop him up on a chair in the window and position yourself opposite. To anybody walking by, you are having a few cans with a good-looking mate!

Credit Card Orders over £50 - pay in 4 monthly payments

Drinkbuddi Travis

UB 563798

£79.95

with legs

£99.95

AS SEEN ON TV

Microwave Bookshelf

This 1.3 metersworth of books embossed with great spines of literature and philosophy makes you look so well read it's almost embarrassing! But this isn't an ordinary shelf of bogus books. Lift up the hinged front and the interior is a fully functioning microwave for heating through pies or what have you. Put it by your bed and wake up to a hot pie!

Microwave Bookshelf

UB 5785498

£299.95

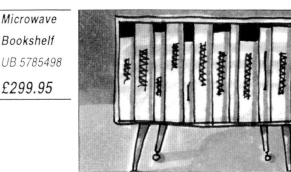

JENNY AGUTTER

You can't buy sex appeal but if you could, JENNY AGUTTER could set up a chain of sex appeal shops (possibly called Sex Appeal Rack) and stock them herself. It was, of course, that sensational transformation between The Railway Children and Walkabout that said it all. She wandered into that tunnel an adolescent teetering on the brink of womanhood, exhausted from having to give Sally Thomsett constant emotional support. She emerged out of that same tunnel into the Australian outback in Walkabout... still the same adolescent teetering on the brink of womanhood, but this time with a less orthodontically wayward sibling. But then she went for a swim, a long, twisting, writhing and - let's not be coy about this - nude swim that seemed to go on for ever, and emerged a woman. Although she pulled herself back into the same white cheesecloth blouse, spiritually, spiritually, she was now wearing the shimmering mantle of a, like, fully mature bird. Academics still argue over whether this is the only time in history when someone has gone to Australia and come back a more mature human being.

Anyway I suppose what we're saying is, wey-hey! but in a nice way. Because there's something delicate about Jennifer. To this day she has the voice of a sixth-former at a posh Surrey school who has just smoked her first packet of Marlboro. She is still in effect juggling two balls - The Girl Ball and the Woman Ball. And as the Girl Ball gets more and more difficult to juggle let us remember Jennifer in that pool in the Outback when she first picked up the Woman Ball and swam with it.

Jimmy Hill

Few people have had such a profound effect on British society as this anvil-faced beardie footy analyser. Almost single-handedly he turned footy from a joyous national pastime into a miserable moan-fest. Week in week out he finds fault in everything and doggedly plugs away with a succession of evermore dull theories that the game is really all about controlling the space in that straight little circle on the edge of the penalty box. Though to our knowledge nobody has agreed with or listened to a single word Jimmy has ever said he has nevertheless continued to try our patience for decades with his whiney voice and bland fashion sense that makes John Major look like Jean-Paul Gaultier.

Unsurprisingly the phrase 'Jimmy Hill' or sometimes 'Jimmy Reckon' together with a stroking motion of the chin, was once commonly used by schoolchildren to denote disbelief in something someone else had just said. It's amazing that Des and Alan don't re-introduce it again to finally chase the Mullah of Misery from our screens forever.

KATARINA WITT

After years of thinking ice-skating was the original Sport Of Queens along came Katarina Witt to introduce a much-needed note of full-blown sex to the proceedings. Well not full full-blown sex obviously as she was out there on her own and none but the hardiest nordic love-muzzle could perform to Olympic standards at those temperatures but as near as damn it anyway.

Though astute sports fans had been tracking her progress up the world rankings for years Katarina really burst onto the international Trouser-Trouble scene with her gold winning see-through costume at the 1988 Winter Olympics (apparently her triple salkoes weren't half bad either). By this and other dazzling acts of athletic eroticism Katarina (or Rina to her friends) made her telling contribution to the end of the Cold War. Remember those shots of all those Beardies pulling at the Berlin Wall? They weren't East Germans trying to get out. They were West Germans trying to get in to see Katarina. Who says a pretty face can't change the course of History?

KEITH RICHARDS

The Emperor of Bad Behaviour, the Dalai Lama of Misconduct, His Unruliness. Keith doesn't need a A to Z to tell him how to behave badly, he just needs some time to himself, a phone and a big box of matches. The thing about Keith is, bad behaviour hasn't spoilt him. Well, it has, but in a good way.

For three decades people have been trying to sum up how Keith looks. Like a shell of a husk of a burnt-out case. Like one of the four horsemen of the Apocalypse, only, like, the least healthy horseman. Or simply: Like a rock star should.

Keith doesn't get tans. Keith doesn't do shopping. Keith doesn't eat food. We imagine a typical day for Keith is: wake up at two in the afternoon, have a cup of tea and a pack of Marlboro in bed. Set fire to bed. Ignore it. Get up, go into one of his nine kitchens, light up something stronger, write brilliant song. Go round to Mick's place. Light up something even stronger. Jerry makes him go outside onto the patio to smoke it. Limo calls. It is so stretched it has a 10-lane bowling alley inside it. Write brilliant song in the back on the way to Wembley Stadium. After gig take eighteen grand's worth of chemical stimulants in as many minutes. Go to bed, or don't.

We want that life. We deserve it.

KYLIE MINOGUE

There are one or two passing references to Kylie in this book, so an explanation may be in order. Kylie, like Felicity Kendal and Kate Moss, is a man's woman. (Meryl Streep, Bette Davis and Cher are women's women, Madonna used to be a woman's woman but is now just a woman again. Cindy Crawford is a man's woman and a woman's woman. It's that complicated.) Women cite most blokes' blind devotion to Kylie as evidence that what they really want is waifs they can treat like feeble teenagers all their lives. Well we're not psychologists, but... what on earth is wrong with that?!

She was born on 28 May 1968. It was the month students clashed with security police on the streets of Paris. How apt that her fourth hit - 'Je ne sais pas pourquoi' - should take inspiration from these events. In the following month, incidentally, prescription charges were introduced in Britain, a subject Kylie has yet to tackle musically.

Born, then, in Melbourne in a time of ferment, she left school at 17 and joined the cast of Neighbours. Interestingly, it is her own name that has become popular the world over, rather than that of her character Charlene. Probably just as well. The world was shocked (explored in her 1990 hit 'Shocked') when she hitched up with INXS guy Michael Hutchence. She pitched up in an episode of the BBC sitcom The Vicar Of Dibley in 1994. And so on.

Let's explode some myths straight away:
"Kylie isn't complicated enough to be interesting." Anyone who has studied the lyrics to 'Got To Be Certain' will know how frighteningly glib that comment is.
"Kylie has never shaken off her squeaky-clean image." Come off it, keep up! She's been stripping off in her videos for years.
"Kylie's voice lets her down." That's pretty rich coming from people who for years have let Bob Dylan get away with singing as though he's got his Walkman on.

So, what's she really like? It may be that, like trying to analyse why you hate Muriel Grey, once you put Kylie under the microscope the whole fragile edifice falls apart. Like Maria in The Sound Of Music she is 'a will o' the wisp'. After hundreds of interviews we still don't know the real Kylie. And maybe that's no bad thing. Perhaps the key to her appeal lies simply in her stonking good looks - clear skin, cheeky mouth, teeth you'd like to suck individually, enigmatic breasts, legs you want to dive between and hair you want to cut off and fashion into a posy for your genitals.

LESLIE ASH

If we're talking icons – and if we're not, let's – we're talking LESLIE ASH. She's gorgeous, she's elfin-faced, and most of us want to throw ourselves at her feet and hug them – however difficult this makes it for her to walk. In 1988 Leslie famously topped a Daily Mirror poll as The Woman Men Would Most Like To Do A Bungee Jump Strapped Together With, narrowly squeezing out Felicity Kendal, we think.

When visiting Brighton, there aren't many men who haven't slipped away from their birds or wives ("I'm just slipping away to buy you a brilliant present" "Oh, alright love") and made the pilgrimage to the alleyway where Leslie was defiled by Phil Daniels in Quadrophenia. We think she should have waited but it was her personal choice and, you know, we accept her reasons.

Leslie's got great hair and she knows how to use it. Will she revert to the classic short blonde look of Cats' Eyes or will she continue to venture into new hair areas, exploring new colour and lengths? Only time will tell.

LIBRARIES

THINGS TO SAY IN A LOUD VOICE IN

- "Do you have 'Blue Penis, Red Penis' by Ray Woodcraft?"

- "Do you have 'Stop. Don't. No. Missus. Listen. Ooh. No.' by the late Frankie Howard?"

- "Can you point me in the direction of your Not Much of A Book But Lots of Descriptions Of Sexual Intercourse section?"

- "Do you have 'I'm Michael Portillo, so you can all just piss off', by Michael Portillo?"

- "What do you mean I have to bring it back?"

- "Do you have 'Call That An Erection?' It's by Ray Woodcraft."

- "You're Jean Daniels and I've come here to spank you."

- "Do you have any TV spin-off books that offer excellent value for money whilst actually enhancing one's enjoyment of the series?"

"BOOKS – HOW DOES THAT WORK THEN?"

LAGER

We'd planned to give you a run-down of how lager is made but in the final analysis we (a) couldn't be arsed to get a book about it and (b) felt that knowing the processes involved might destroy the mystical aura that surrounds the Beautiful Beverage. We're guessing but it probably involves boiling up some hops and barley in a big vat and leaving to cool, stirring occasionally with a huge paddle thing.

Johnny Ruskie sips vodka, Italians like girly Martinis, French guys insist pathetically on drinking wine. The national drink of Burma is pigs' urine. It's a funny old world out there. If we didn't have so much on we'd pack a suitcase full of cans and go out into the world as lager missionaries, distributing samples and spreading word of the healing powers of hops and the very real hope of salvation through God's Lager.

Lager brands.

Pick a brand of lager at random, stick with it and champion it with complete, unrelenting, blind devotion. Claim automatically that all other brands taste like they've been strained through a Bolivian tobacco worker's pants (see Gnats Piss and Pants). If anyone criticises your chosen brew you have to ask them to step outside as, basically, this is as serious as being accused of cheating at poker or enjoying the company of your parents. This means unfortunately that you have to defend your brand's TV advert, even if you think it's a load of old unfunny toss fronted by an utter fuck-wit.

Lager Names

Unlike Spades you must never call lager by its real name. Instead one of a range of jokey nicknames will help fill those awkward silences that can so often occur between opening time and chucking out.

1. Australian Neck-oil (Antipodean brews only)
2. Senior Tizer (Universal)
3. Kaiserwasser, or, Himmler's Choice(German sounding lager
4. Falling down/throwing-up water
5. A Pint Of The Old Gold 'n' Cold

Bubbling Under, Golden Syrup, "Curry Sauce", the Wonder Stuff, Big Yellow , etc. Note: only a complete prat i.e. someone who works in advertising, would think of asking for a pint of 'Amber Nectar'.

Enjoy your lager-drinking, but be aware of the following potential hazards:

Politically-correct lager

As in so many other aspects of blokeish life-style, lager is under threat from the sadly misguided pollitically-correct lobby. PC lager is no fun at all, being non-alcoholic and serve served in a re-cycled glass bottle with a poncey wedge of organically grown lime. If offered this liquid insult, the only possible course of action is to refuse loudly, and request the perfect alternative, i.e. a paralytically-correct lager, such as Carlsberg Special Brew.

Other Beers (which, unbelievably, aren't lager)

Real ale - avoid this at all costs. One sip and you turn into someone who looks and talks like a geography teacher.
Surreal ale - more awful rubbish, with the added drawbacks of burning giraffes, fish and melting watches.
Stout and Bitter - probably how you'll end up, if you insist on drinking either.

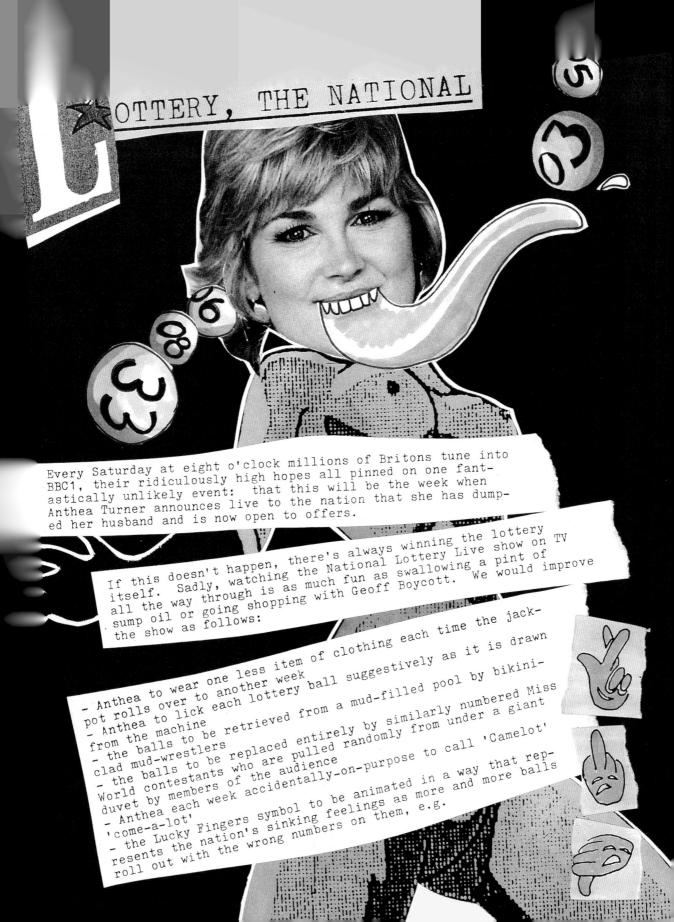

Every Saturday at eight o'clock millions of Britons tune into BBC1, their ridiculously high hopes all pinned on one fant-astically unlikely event: that this will be the week when Anthea Turner announces live to the nation that she has dump-ed her husband and is now open to offers.

If this doesn't happen, there's always winning the lottery itself. Sadly, watching the National Lottery Live show on TV all the way through is as much fun as swallowing a pint of sump oil or going shopping with Geoff Boycott. We would improve the show as follows:

- Anthea to wear one less item of clothing each time the jack-pot rolls over to another week
- Anthea to lick each lottery ball suggestively as it is drawn from the machine
- the balls to be retrieved from a mud-filled pool by bikini-clad mud-wrestlers
- the balls to be replaced entirely by similarly numbered Miss World contestants who are pulled randomly from under a giant duvet by members of the audience
- Anthea each week accidentally-on-purpose to call 'Camelot' 'come-a-lot'
- the Lucky Fingers symbol to be animated in a way that rep-resents the nation's sinking feelings as more and more balls roll out with the wrong numbers on them, e.g.

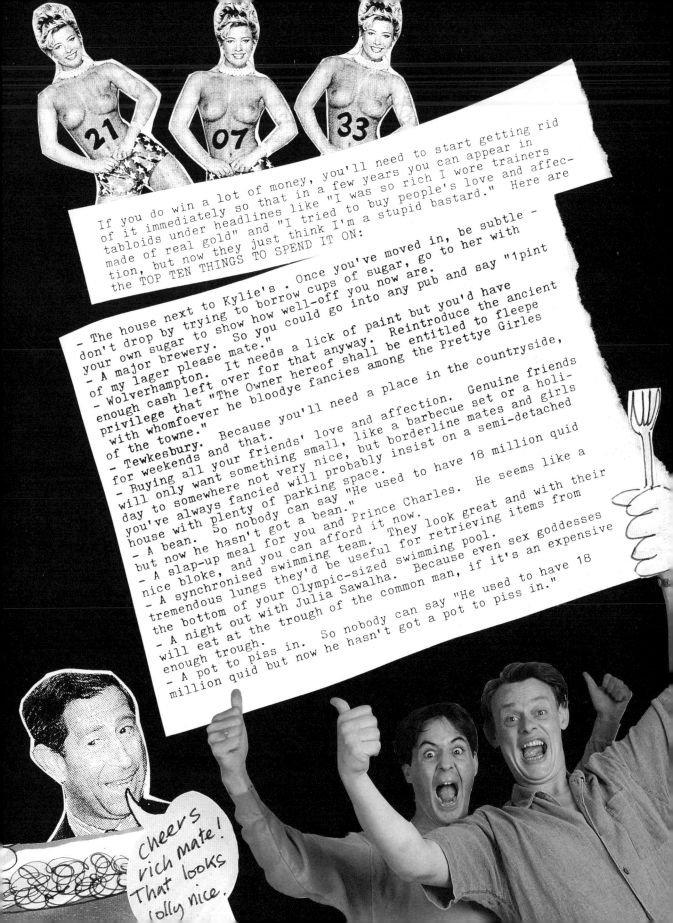

If you do win a lot of money, you'll need to start getting rid of it immediately so that in a few years you can appear in tabloids under headlines like "I was so rich I wore trainers made of real gold" and "I tried to buy people's love and affection, but now they just think I'm a stupid bastard." Here are the TOP TEN THINGS TO SPEND IT ON:

- The house next to Kylie's. Once you've moved in, be subtle - don't drop by trying to borrow cups of sugar, go to her with your own sugar to show how well-off you now are.
- A major brewery. So you could go into any pub and say "1pint of my lager please mate."
- Wolverhampton. It needs a lick of paint but you'd have enough cash left over for that anyway. Reintroduce the ancient privilege that "The Owner hereof shall be entitled to fleepe with whomfoever he bloodye fancies among the Prettye Girles of the towne."
- Tewkesbury. Because you'll need a place in the countryside, for weekends and that. Genuine friends will only want something small, like a barbecue set or a holiday to somewhere not very nice, but borderline mates and girls you've always fancied will probably insist on a semi-detached house with plenty of parking space.
- A bean. So nobody can say "He used to have 18 million quid but now he hasn't got a bean."
- A slap-up meal for you and Prince Charles. He seems like a nice bloke, and you can afford it now.
- A synchronised swimming team. They look great and with their tremendous lungs they'd be useful for retrieving items from the bottom of your Olympic-sized swimming pool.
- A night out with Julia Sawalha. Because even sex goddesses will eat at the trough of the common man, if it's an expensive enough trough.
- A pot to piss in. So nobody can say "He used to have 18 million quid but now he hasn't got a pot to piss in."

Cheers rich mate! That looks jolly nice.

LEAVING CARDS, FUN WITH

It's always a bit of an upset when someone leaves an office to work elsewhere. If they were a GOOD MATE, you've got to find someone new to fax photocopies of your arse to, or cover for you when you've taken the afternoon off, but left your jacket on the back of the your chair so it looks like you've just popped out to the coffee machine. If, however, they were a COMPLETE PRAT, it's even more of a loss. Now who will become the butt of all those practical jokes that make a crap job halfway bearable? Same too for birds. Losing a GOOD-LOOKING OFFICE BIRD can be a tragedy, particularly if they were of the short-skirt-always-bending-over-the-lowest-drawer-of-the-filing-cabinet-type. Losing an UGLY BIRD is even more of a problem - now who's going to actually run the office? And, besides, snogging the ugly bird is the only true test of extreme, gale force drunkesnness at the office Christmas Party.

Fortunately, when people leave you get leaving-dos by way of compensation. A last, inebriated chance to tell someone what you really think of them or to make one final attempt to get into their knickers - only to find next morning that they aren't leaving, as such, merely being promoted to head office, with direct responsibility for your salary and prospects. Oh dear...

That's why Leaving Cards present much safer opportunities for Bad Behaviour : you can write what you like in them - offensive, salacious, or otherwise - and you don't have to do it in your own handwriting or even sign your own name. Just imagine, you can create all sorts of fun simply by writing 'I always fancied the arse off you. Call me', followed by your boss's home phone number.

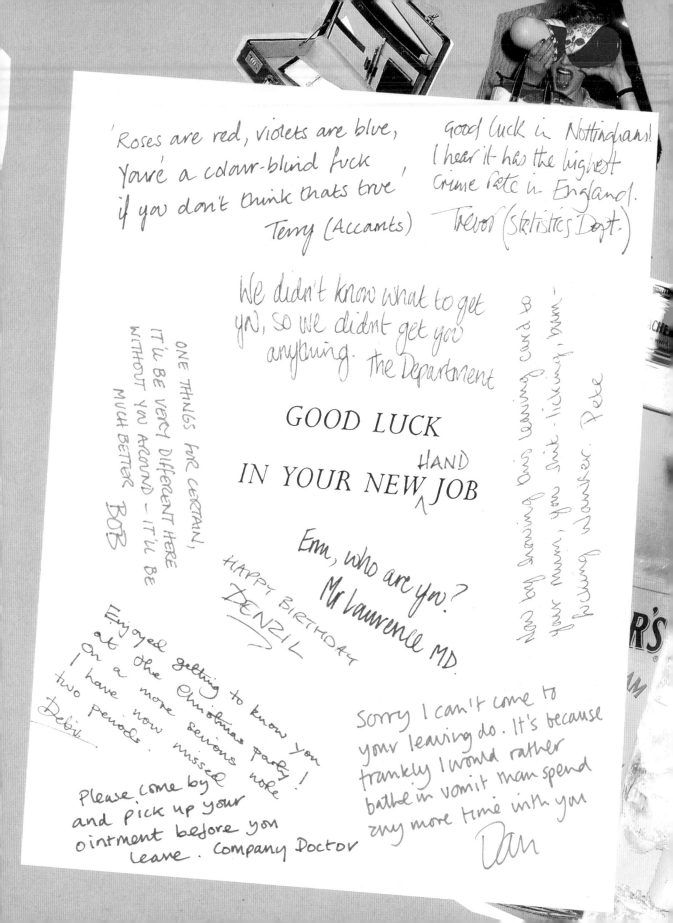

'Roses are red, violets are blue,
You're a colour-blind fuck
if you don't think thats true'
Terry (Accounts)

Good luck in Nottingham!
I hear it has the highest
crime rate in England.
Trevor (Statistics Dept.)

We didn't know what to get
you, so we didn't get you
anything. The Department

ONE THINGS FOR CERTAIN,
IT'LL BE VERY DIFFERENT HERE
WITHOUT YOU AROUND – IT'LL BE
MUCH BETTER
BOB

GOOD LUCK

IN YOUR NEW HAND JOB

HAPPY BIRTHDAY
DENZIL

Emm, who are you?
Mr Laurence MD.

Now by signing this leaving card to
your mum, you shit-licking, bum-
fucking wanker. Pete

Enjoyed getting to know you
at the Christmas Party!
On a more serious note
I have now missed
two periods.
Debi.

Please come by
and pick up your
ointment before you
leave. Company Doctor

Sorry I can't come to
your leaving do. It's because
frankly I would rather
bathe in vomit than spend
any more time with you
Dan

MORNING AFTER, The.

Generally speakin when it comes to BEHAVING BADLY it's not a particularly great idea to hang around the scene of the crime too long afterwards. Whether your bad behaiour has in- volved several people...

(PARTY CRIME)

...or just one (SEX CRIME)

...the most tactful thing to do is withdraw as quickly as possible afterwards whilst they're still reeling from what you've done and therefore less likely to press charges.

If, for some reason like a coma or rampant sexual optimism you fail to do this then you will wake to find yourself in the perilous uncharted waters known as....The Morning After.

The first thing to say if this happens is...

Name Daphr
Address (Mey)
0177
Tel: Marbe
10
Name
Address Buck
Tel: 01
Name
Address
2060212

DO NOT PANIC

...It probably won't be the first time someone has woken up on the floor of a perfect stranger's bedroom covered in stale lager and cigarette ash with a broken yucca in one hand and someone's left tit in the other - though it may be the last if the tit in question turns out to be a male one. The main thing to remember is the following simple rules, most of which have been tested in real life.

1 WHATEVER YOU DO <u>don't</u> have a wash or a shower. However disgusting you might feel now you'll feel ten times worse when you get back into your clothes. Besides wasn't it you who was sick in the bath last night?

2 WHATEVER YOU DO <u>don't</u> offer to help clean up. This will only tie you in further to the mess and give people longer to remember all the horrible and disgusting things you did the night before.

3 WHATEVER YOU DO <u>don't</u> tell anyone your real name. Either make one up or start answering to whatever name you're called by first. This will serve to avoid complications and unnecessary legal expenses later.

4 WHATEVER YOU DO <u>do</u> leave by the nearest available exit as quietly and as quickly as possible. Do not stop for toast or coffee. Do not collect addresses, even from pretty girls looking gorgeous and sleepy in men's pyjamas. Just smile, wave and, with the casual look of someone who's just popping out to fetch the papers, be on your way as soon as possible. Go on. Oh alright. You can take her address but nobody else's...

MANDIES

Every Romeo needs his Juliet, every yin its yan. The man who is planning on Behaving Badly neglects Mandies at his peril.

Mandies are young, extrovert working-class city girls with permed, corkscrew blonde hair. They live in shops by day and fun-pubs by night. They wear tight skirts and multi-coloured tops in non-natural fibres. They like dancing and only ever drink sweet shorts like Taboo and Cadburys Chocolate Eclair. They like a 'good laugh', pinching men's bottoms and smoking menthol cigar-ettes. Though shy and prudish when sober when they get drunk they go like the wind and even the most sexually inadequate man stands a fair-to-middling chance of a tongue-sandwich if he's within range when Bryan Adams comes on.

Like many of the best things in life Mandies are best appreci-ated young - between the ages of 15 and 18 - when they're at their most uncomplicated and sexy. For these few brief years they are usually loud, outrageous, hilarious, earthy, spontan-eous and fantastically sexually corruptible. By the time they hit 19 though strange things start to happen: they get promo-tion at Boots, start to talk like their mothers, take themselves very seriously. Even more ominously if you so much as brush past them on the way to the bar they act as though you've been engaged forever and a day and you can find yourself studying the 'Pronuptia' catalogue in the blink of an eye and deciding between peach and avocado bathroom suites for your Wimpey Starter home.

Still when that happens it's just onto the next batch of GCSE candidates isn't it? One of the best things you can do with a Mandy is dance with her really smuttily, buy her a large Cuba Libra, make a clumsy attempt to snog her, succeed, and then tearfully confess that you're gay. This course of act-ion can have three possible results.

1) She thinks you're joking and shags your brains out.
2) She thinks you're totally serious and still shags your brains out.
3) She goes to fetch her big brother Darren.

Of course not all of these options are as much fun as each other.

MANDIES
THE MALE EQUIVALENT: Darrens

The male equivalent of Mandies. Unlike Mandies Darrens have no part to play in your life of Bad Behaviour and are to be avoided like the plague - especially if they've got a broken pils bottle in one hand and are saying things like "So, Mr Smart-arse. What was it that you said again?".

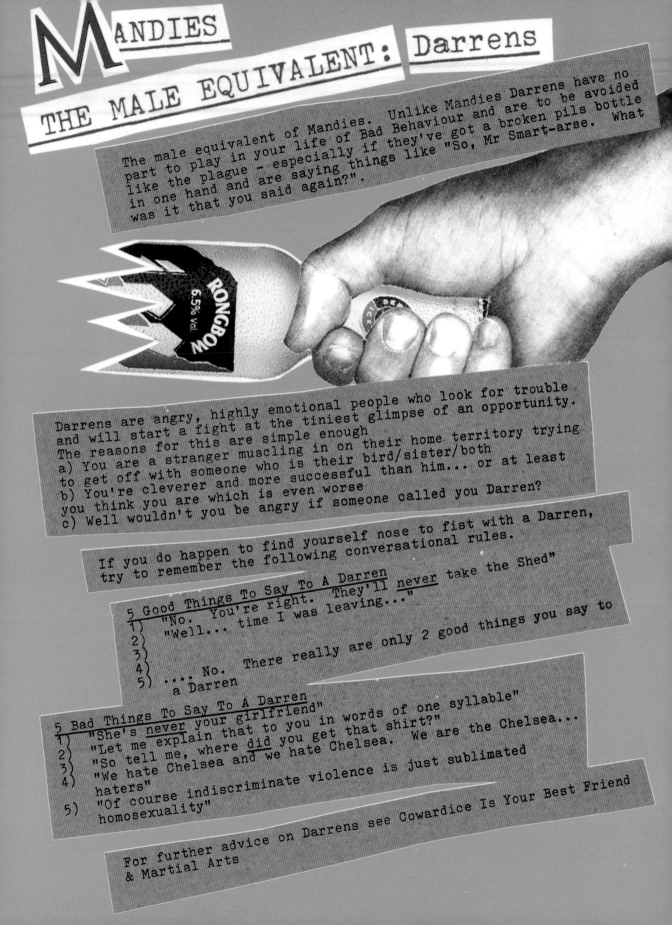

Darrens are angry, highly emotional people who look for trouble and will start a fight at the tiniest glimpse of an opportunity. The reasons for this are simple enough
a) You are a stranger muscling in on their home territory trying to get off with someone who is their bird/sister/both
b) You're cleverer and more successful than him... or at least you think you are which is even worse
c) Well wouldn't you be angry if someone called you Darren?

If you do happen to find yourself nose to fist with a Darren, try to remember the following conversational rules.

5 Good Things To Say To A Darren
1) "No. You're right. They'll never take the Shed"
2) "Well... time I was leaving..."
3)
4) .... No. There really are only 2 good things you say to
5) a Darren

5 Bad Things To Say To A Darren
1) "She's never your girlfriend"
2) "Let me explain that to you in words of one syllable"
3) "So tell me, where did you get that shirt?"
4) "We hate Chelsea and we hate Chelsea. We are the Chelsea... haters"
5) "Of course indiscriminate violence is just sublimated homosexuality"

For further advice on Darrens see Cowardice Is Your Best Friend & Martial Arts

MARTIAL ARTS

Behaving Badly has its perils and its a sad fact of life that not everybody will be as amused or moved by your brave deeds as you are. It's a good idea therefore to prepare for the worst by acquainting yourself with a few basics of self-defence. Obviously, in an ideal world, we would all already have our black belts, fifth dan, having had the shite kicked out of us for years in a draughty church hall by a three foot tall oriental psychopath but never mind; there's plenty you can do.

There are three basic martial art moves you need to know: the Block the Throw and the Roll.

THE BLOCK.

Look your enemy in the eye. As he makes his move, turn, grab hold of something large and heavy and chuck it at him. NB Experience suggests that some objects are not ideal for this. Empty matchboxes, dirty tea towels and half pints of anything other than sulphuric acid should not be used as they tend only to goad your enemy into jumping even harder on your head.

THE THROW.

Look your enemy in the eye.As he makes his move, turn,grab hold of something large and heavy and chuck it at him. NB Experience suggests that some objects are not ideal for this. Half empty matchboxes,dirty tea towels and half pints of anything other than sulphuric acid should not be used as they tend only to goad your enemy into jumping even harder on your head.

THE ROLL

Look your enemy in the eye.As he makes his move, turn and grab your own throat,feigning a sudden fit or seizure.Fall to the floor and,thrashing around,roll away from danger. NB Try to roll away from rather than towards your enemy as this gives you more chance of effecting a clean getaway.This move isn't recommended if you're out in someone else's shirt.

As an alternative to these moves you could simply practise the even more ancient Italian art of Chaio. This involves facing your enemy, giving him a slightly leery smile, a little wave and legging it away as fast as your legs can carry you.Though this may seem a little low on the macho scale if you do it often enough you'll quickly find it has a certain dignified charm all of its own.

Music has four main functions in a Bloke's life. We use it as:

a) Something to mess about to and annoy the neighbours. This is the only possible explanation for the popularity of Motorhead.
b) A pulling/sex soundtrack. This is especially true of ambient/ trance outfits whose work sends women into a state of such lassitude and apathy they can't be bothered not to sleep with you.
c) A means of defining our social status and tribal belonging. Were it not for such arbitrary distinctions as Thrash Metal, Soft Metal and Soft Thrash how on earth would millions of teenage males know who their friends should be?
d) A way of saying things you can't say. Without music how could Blokes express unexpressible feelings like love, social aliention and vaguely homo-erotic yearnings for men in skin-tight satin trousers?

YOUR RECORD COLLECTION

Apart from a few old favourites, you never actually listen to any of the several odd thousand albums you have stacked in the corner of your bedroom. No, what you do is sit on the floor with the radio on and memorise every word on the covers. After all, some day it might come in handy to just know that the nice crunchy bit on AC/DC's 'Whole Lotta Rosy' was played on a Gibson Thunderbird fretless guitar.

NEW BANDS TO TELL CHICS YOU LIKE

A long and mostly fictitious list that should include such names as Blur, Oasis, Pulp, Elastica, Tricky and A Guy Called Gerald. If your busy life as a young and thrusting executive means that you've never actually listened to them, the following simple formula will stand you in good stead: "Yeah I know they're not The Kinks but then again no one ever was - not even 'The Kinks'. By the time she's worked this one out you'll be long gone off down the offie to get milk for her herbal tea.

OLD BANDS YOU MUST NEVER TELL CHICS YOU LIKE EVEN IF YOU DO

Yes, Jethro Tull, Mike Oldfield, Genesis, The Grateful Dead, Whitesnake, UFO or Marillion. Though you may still love them no girl worth her salt wants to be seen with anyone who still so obviously has the tastes of an introverted suburban 70's fifteen year old.

MODELS

Models are not of this world but extraordinary creatures from another planet where people spend all day waxing their bikini line and trying to cop off with someone from U2. Though most of us are very unlikely to ever come into close contact with them it's always as well to be prepared with a few conversational lines just in case you win the lottery or get that unexpected England call-up.

FIVE GOOD THINGS TO SAY TO A MODEL

1. Gosh. You've lost so much weight.
2. Do you agree that this season brown is the new red?
3. You really ought to be a film star.
4. Travelling first class around the world must be such a bore.
5. No, actually I really like lettuce

FIVE BAD THINGS TO SAY TO A MODEL

1. Do you fancy a plate of chips?
2. Were you the one who went out with Rod Stewart?
3. Have you read the new Gabriel-Garcia Marquez novel ?
4. My Mum buys all my clothes from the Grattons catalogue.
5. Do you feel any guilt or sense of responsibility for the number of girls suffering from anorexia?

When discussing models with your girlfriend never, EVER say or do anything to indicate you might find them remotely attractive. Say things like "If she put on a couple of stone she'd be alright" and "I bet she's got skin like a lunar landing site". Of course she won't believe a word but as in all these things it's not what you say that counts it's the fact that you said it.

As any astute watcher of society knows the 80's myth of the New Man has now been kicked into touch once and for all, along with the fiction that size doesn't matter and the delusion that talking about your mortgage to people you meet at parties is any way socially acceptable.

Instead of the New Man we now have another label - THE NEW LAD - a crude caricature of masculinity that says that all men are really interested in his footie, lager and full length posters of Pamela Anderson in a see through swimming cossie. This is total bollocks. Everyone knows that Pamela's cossies- though wet and clingy enough-are almost impossible to see through without the aid of an electron microscope

However... The New Man syndrome can be a useful area to explore when you are hunting game. If you're with a girl and you feel it's absolutely necessary to show you can temper your testosterone-you might want to try at least two of the following

keep a pint of skimmed milk in your fridge at all times (looks health conscious - remember, she is bound to be on a diet)

read 'I Know Why The Caged Bird Sings' by Maya Angelou and recite stanzas whilst doing the washing up.   weep at BBC costume dramas

learn the names of at least three types of plant

try seeing things from their angle   cook
-sit down to pee f'instance

brake when you see old people at
a pedestrian crossing   watch Masterchef

WARNING: you may now grow breasts
if you keep the charade up too long

NAT'S PISS

General term for any brand of lager that isn't the one you drink.It's traditional to accompany your use of the word by screwing up your face with disgust and horror, then shaking your head and sighing deeply in sympathy for the poor bastards who have to drink it.For fans of British Regional Racism Nat's Piss offers an ideal opportunity to score cheap and easy points against your favourite target group-Northerners,Southerners, Mancs,Brummies or even Glaswegians.The only exception to this is the Welsh whose lager is universally acknowledged to be shite beyond all hope of redemption.

Interestingly enough scientists have calculated that it would take the average Nat sixtythree years and four days to fill a pint glass with piss, assuming of course that it wasn't a hot day and its little efforts didn't evaporate in the sun before they could be measured.

NELLIE KIM

Soviet gymnast from the late 70's whose main distinction was that in a crowded market of flat-chested eleven year olds she was the only one who you could admit to fancying out loud without anyone calling the police. Though she rarely won the hearts of the Olympic judges Nellie always got straight tens from the lads over here, who were won over by a combination of her elegant floor-work and her dazzlingly developed baps. A recent count between us established a total of over fifty-eight seperate sexual fantasies starring Nellie Kim, only six of which did not involve the parallel bars in one shape or form

NEW JOB

Starting a new job is, we all know, an incredibly difficult and stressful thing. One minute you're cock of the walk, in tune with every gag and nuance, master of all you survey. The next you're a stuttering, nervous wreck who smiles too much and can't even find your way to the toilet without throwing yourself at the mercy of the kind of swamp-life you wouldn't have been seen dead talking to in your old place. It's all very dull. Help is at hand though if you remember the following invaluable rules.

1/ Don't try too hard. Wandering around shaking everyone's hand and making energetic efforts to get to know everyone is a recipe for disaster and before you know it you'll be trapped in the canteen with the Office Sad thumbing through her holiday photos and saying 'lovely' a lot. Much better to keep your cool and cultivate no more than a polite interest in what's going on around you. Let them worry about what you think of <u>them</u> and before you know it all the top dogs will be jostling to take you out for a post-work pint.

2/ Don't go on about your old job and what a laugh you used to have with Danny and John in Data Management as most people:
a) Couldn't give a toss about someone they've never met
b) Will automatically assume that if the last place was so great the only reason you left was because you were sacked for fiddling the staff Christmas fund.

Instead make your new colleagues feel good about themselves by saying your last place was hell on earth and that you only just managed to escape with your sanity and reputation intact. Of course this does not apply if you <u>were</u> sacked for fiddling the staff Christmas fund when you should probably say you spent the last five years as a cowboy in ~~the~~ Bolivia.

3/ Make and receive loads of personal calls. This will:
a) Mark you out as a successful person with an active and varied social life
b) Establish that you're very much your own man and won't be cowed into giving up your whole life to the company.

Of course if you are in a company where everyone makes personal calls all the time then phoning the same mate twenty times to check on the cricket score might not be so powerful a statement of individuality after all and you'll have to get your mate to use a host of different names and accents if you don't want to be written off as a Johnny No Friends.

OFFICE POLITICS

Office politics is of paramount importance to the well-being of the British economy, but it is a dangerous game and if you are going to play it, it's well to acquaint yourself with some of the key players in the corporate jungle. When it comes to work all idea of human complexity breaks down and people always conform to one of the following readily xxxxxxxx identifiable stereotypes.

1 THE WHINGER

To the dedicated Whinger everything but everything is a problem, Seeing as how they will never be happy anyway don't waste any time being nice with them but get in there from the word go and make their life hell. Kill off their plants, steal their stationary, unplug their phone, put a dead bulb in their swivel lamp - the possibilities for the worst kind of Bad Behaviour are endless, especially as, when all's said and done, the Whinger secretly enjoys being miserable.

2 THE LOSER

A sad and tragic individual who, for a reason no one can quite put their finger on, has become the sacrificial lamb to everyone's inner turmoils and frustrations. Because of this Losers are always desperate to please, which should provide endless opportunities for gratuitous acts of cruelty like eating all their sandwiches or getting them to come in at the weekend to do all your work for you. Though it's a good idea to let a Loser think they are your friend - try not to get too close to them or everyone will think you're a Loser too. Remember Losers are a disease and you're only being cruel to be kind. OK cruel to be cruel but what the hell.

3 THE HEAD PREFECT

Every office has a goody-two-shoes, a desperate inadequate who's under the illusion that by creeping up to the boss and doing everything in their best handwriting they'll go further in life than you. Unfortunately they are usually right. It's generally unwise to take Head Prefects on directly, instead laugh loudly at everything they say, take copious notes when they give instructions, offer them your sweets. Deprived of a reason to pick on you they will go quickly mad and do something they regret at the next bi-monthly get together over cheese and wine.

4 THE ASSASSIN

This is a distant and dangerous cousin of the Head Prefect. Though they seem to be one of the gang they are actually a dark satanic force working ceaselessly for your destruction. The best way to identify one is by bitching about someone you really like. If they join in they're definitely Assassins. If they walk away in disgust they probably think you are. As Assassins are famously great memo writers, ~~juicy~~ why not get on the company E-mail and, totally by accident, send a nice, juicy series of sexual fantasies and snide comments about peoples appearances from their terminal? Now that really is a lot of fun.

5 THE SEX POT

This really has nothing to do with Office Politics except in the unlikely event that anything starts to happen between you and her every other male in the whole building will turn their fire on you and try to shoot you down in flames. Still, that shouldn't stop you bouncing around her desk like a demented puppy or fixing the seating plan on the company day out so you get to sit next to her all the way to Lego-World and back. As for actually sleeping with someone you work with this is only ever a bad idea if... no, it's never a bad idea.

$\underline{\text{OLD GIRLFRIENDS}}$

Old Girlfriends are a distinctly modern phenomenon. In the old days – as anyone who's ever watched Terry And June can testify – people used to take a Stalinist approach to such things and happily airbrushed their former birds out of history with the gay abandon of old Joe going to work on his photo collection of former political allies. Nowadays this is only done by birds who, as they do in all things, are brutally pragmatic about their past, developing the kind of selective amnesia that leads to them all – however rampant – maintaining that you are only the third bloke they've ever slept with.

Blokes though have a much harder time trying to lay our old ghosts. Being instinctively generous and faithful creatures we hate letting go of our past and will find almost any excuse to keep our Old Girlfriends on file and still in the loop. Men, after all, are naturally optimistic creatures and deep in the souls find it impossible to accept that what's done really $\underline{\text{is}}$ done and that they really have seen that incredible trick with the Cadbury's white chocolate finger and the bowl of whipped cream for the very last time.

So much for the theory, what about the practicalities of seeing your Old Girlfriend and getting away with it with the New Girl-friend. This is a difficult trick to pull off and will require all the tact, sensitivity and lying skills you can muster. It isn't impossible though if you follow the following five golden rules.

1 Don't make your life any harder than it already is by imagining for one single second second that your New Girlfriend won't be jealous of your old one. Remember most birds have been Old Girlfriends too at some time in their career and know from personal experience that a quick shag for old times sake is always on the cards when two people who've exchanged intimate juices meet again in a public place.

2 If your New Girlfriend makes a big song and dance of your meeting up with your Old Girlfriend why not call her bluff and invite her along. She of course will refuse, leaving you home and dry on the moral high ground. Try not to smirk when this happens or you may find you might not be allowed to go after all.

3 Try to think of a good reason to see your Old Girlfriend, especially if your relationship with her ended without recourse to lawyers and/or physical violence on either side. Good reasons include:

a) You need to get your Best of Barry White CD back
b) She's your boss and you'll probably get fired if you turn up for work
c) She's got the other half of your winning National lottery ticket

Bad reasons for wanting to see your Old Girlfriend include:
a) She's just split up with someone and is having a really hard time
b) You just can't live without her recipe for chicken with cashew nuts
c) You'd like a night out with a girl who drinks pints

4 Whatever you do NEVER compare your old Girlfriend with your New Girlfriend. This is her job and she will resent it bitterly if you try to do it for her. If seeing your old Girlfriend reminds you of a position you used to do together that you haven't yet done with the New One do not under any circumstances say so. Coming home half-pissed with a brand new sexual agenda is as sure a way as any of being a single man in the morning.

5 If you find that you are seeing a lot of your Old Girlfriend consider the possibility that maybe after all you made the wrong choice. Dump your New Girlfriend and start going out with your Old Girlfriend. Strangely enough this will make your Old Girlfriend your New Girlfriend and your New Girlfriend your Old Girlfriend. If this doesn't confuse you too much you can start the whole thing rolling again from square one.

RAL, Sex.

See under Grant, Hugh

and In Your Dreams Old Son.

PANTS

Women like to think that we men are very casual about our pants, putting on the first pair that comes to hand in the morning and wearing them until the man from the council comes round to take them away in a sealed plastic bag. Nothing could be further from the truth. Pants are amazingly important things to blokes and we run our grunty drawer with all the care and attention of Terry Venables looking after the England Squad, only with even more Home and International success. We therefore feel very well placed to offer the definitive guide to these most vital of garments.

PANT TYPES
There are four main types of Pant:-

EVERYDAY PANTS
These are strong solid performers that, in their own unspectacular way, get the job done without calling too much attention to themselves. Being solid and unspectacular they can be worn without undue problems for anything up to ten years after which they automatically become Emergency Pants. Every man should have at least four pairs of Everyday Pants preferably in a range of colours to aid identification and give long-term girlfriends an illusion of variety.

DATE PANTS
These are vital to the task of psyching yourself up for that first big grandstand occasion with a brand new bird. They are either brand new versions of whatever it is you have as Everyday Pants or something entirely different from another, unfamiliar Pant genre. Good Date Pants give you that air of danger and confidence that can prove such a turn on to women. Bad Date Pants, on the other hand, can be a total disaster especially if they give you a rash or make you walk like someone who's just spent a fortnight riding bare-back across the Rocky Mountains.

(If you find a pair that works for you try not to wear them every time you meet your women as their special quality can soon diminish and you'll quickly end up with just another pair of Everyday Pants on your hands.)

LUCKY PANTS
The equivalent of Billy's Boots these are highly-charged garments that you pull out to help you through times of real crisis like job or DHSS interviews, driving tests or that once-in-seven -years visit to the dentist. As Lucky Pants are generally ancient and fading hangovers from school days they should never be worn as Date Pants, as most girls are strangly unimpressed by the sight of a man in 70's-style purple Y's that are three sizes too small.

EMERGENCY PANTS These are a motley collection of previous Everyday, Date or Lucky Pants that, though they've long gone past all hope of useful wear are kept on stand-by at the very back of your grunty drawer if all else fails. As well as providing a useful fall-back position Emergency Pants also act like a three dimensional photo-album, allowing you to recall instantly the various triumphs and disasters that occurred while they were in active service. For this reason alone Emergency Pants are to be guarded with your life against girlfriends/wives/mothers who having no pants nostalgia themselves (girls are notoriously unsentimental about their kecks) try to rob us boys of our most cherished memories.

PANTS STYLES

Y-fronts. Y-front Men are usually seen as solid and conservative citizens who, by their choice of these most unsexy of all garments, are making a bold bid for the underpantal high moral ground. Deep down though Y-front Men are deeply insecure and frightened, which is why they need the re-assurance of all that extra material and no-nonsense gusset work to see them through the day.

Slips. Slip Men are the poor relations of the pants family as the sad fact that almost nobody looks good in them becomes clearer and clearer as the years go by. It wasn't always so - as anyone who's seen re-runs of Bouquet Of Barbed Wire can tell you - but the days when tight clingy male knickers were the definition of sex on a stick are now long gone. Nowadays Slips are strictly for people with no personal vanity and/or Dennis Waterman fans.

Boxers. Back in the 80's Boxers ruled the Pant world as men rushed to re-position themselves as stylish individuals with a taste for pure cotton and freedom. These days though Boxer Men are more on the defensive as the fad for wearing what were no more than thin PE shorts under your trousers quickly turned into yesterdays Pant news. Still, girls really do prefer them to Slips or Y-fronts and thanks to a combination of air circulation and narrower humid area they can be worn again and again without much danger.

G-Strings/Thongs. These are not advisable unless you're a fifty-six year old Frenchman on a Club Med holiday. It has to be said that outside the sporting and showbiz worlds most girls first reaction on seeing either will be to call the Police.

PANT COLOURS

This is a matter of taste and style. The only exception to this is brown which, unless you have some kind of death wish, you will never EVER allow to darken your Pants drawer again.

White is clean, virginal and sexy. Can be dangerous though if you're not a tanned and muscly Brad Pitt look-a-like or your toilet habits are not of Olympic standard.

Red is a tricky one. On the one hand it's bold and self-confident, sending out all sorts of unconscious signals of dangerous animal passion and bull-like potency. On the other hand it's highly visible and any errors of styling or maintenance will be glaringly exposed. To be avoided if your grunties are intern-ational standard.

Blue and Green are generally a safe bet as they go well with most duvets and help to bring out the colour of your eyes. Try to avoid lime green though as having a bird throw up all over you at the moment of passion can be more than a little off-putting.

Black is fine as long as the Pants in question are cotton. Anything too silky and birds will just think you go around all day in your swimming cozie.

Patterns/Stripes are dodgy as they can very easily make you look like a little boy and/or someone who buys his pants from markets. This doesn't apply to Boxers where almost anything goes unless they're novelty ones when great care has to be taken not to wear the wrong thing at the wrong time. Whipping off your trousers to reveal a pair with Italia 90 on them can make you look very sad indeed.

SHOULD I CHANGE MY PANTS EVERY DAY?

Of course not. What do you want to do, give us all a bad name? Research has shown that, except for during a World Cup or for the first fortnight of some-one buying a new washing machine, men get at least three whole days out of an average pair of pants before putting them into a wash.

It's important that you explain to girls that the reason we do this is nothing to do with laziness and everything to do with the fact that men have an emot-ional relationship with our pants. Like most rela-tionships this has to be worked at by close, daily contact. Choosing to wear a pair of pants again is an act of loyalty and friendship – rather like choos-ing to see the same mate three nights running or going to the same pub to drink the same lager – and as such is to be respected rather than derided.

THE PUB

Pubs are the Churches of the Bloke's life, except of course we don't just go into them for weddings and funerals and you don't have to kneel down quite as often. To us, they're nevertheless places of worship and quiet contemplation where you can go to escape from the stresses and strains of daily life and have exactly the same argument with your mates as you did the last time you went there.

However, like all things spiritual, the Pub is coming under attack from mis-guided modernisers and people with marketing degrees from New Universities who want to turn them into clean, comfortable 'leisure environments' that appeal to everyone, including children and women. This, though laudable in some ways - a few more chics anywhere never go amiss - it's entirely mis-guided in others. In our book, Blokes simply don't want to do their drinking in continental-style cafes with wicker chairs and Celine Dion on the sound-system. No, they want their pubs old, dark, dirty and as depressing as the EastEnders Christmas Special so you can cheer yourself up by getting off your face on 12 pints of falling-down liquid.

THE LANDLORD

Variously known as the Licensee, Mine Host and the fat drunken bastard with terminal halitosis, the Landlord is the heart through which the life-blood of any drinking establishment flows. In a trade that's essentially remained unchanged since medieval times, his task is to discharge the ancient rites of roadside hospitality and fulfil such important powers and responsibilities as providing hearty vitals for weary travellers and taking sole charge of the volume control when England V Wales comes on the tele.

Bearing this in mind, it's no surprise that so many Blokes will do almost anything to get on the right side of the Landlord - buy him drinks, laugh at his jokes, fetch their own glasses from the tables etc... This is fine as a damage limitation exercise but can be a bad idea if you think for one moment that doing any of it will mean that the Landlord actually likes you as a result. This is what's known as Regular's Fallacy - the curious belief that because you've sat on your arse at the same bar for donkey's years guzzling the family fortune you've somehow got a say in the running of the place. THIS IS JUST NOT TRUE and if you ever hear yourself uttering such phrases as "You know what you should do George" or "No, not another Kiwi barmaid" you should seek psychiatric help straight away.

Still you've got to say something to your Landlord as he's pouring the slops tray into your glass, so to help you we've compiled another handy list.

5 GOOD THINGS TO SAY TO A LANDLORD

1. Oh... and have one for yourself
2. No, I don't mind coins...
3. Yeah, bloody Belgians telling us what flavour crisps we can eat
4. I hear the new bloke at the Dog & Parrot's a total loser
5. No, a dirty dimple mug with a chipped handle's absolutely fine

5 BAD THINGS TO SAY TO A LANDLORD

1. How much?
2. Can you change a fifty?
3. No, actually the European Community is good for Britain
4. I saw this cracking bird in the Dog & Parrot last night
5. No. I think I did say I wanted a straight glass

THE ROUND

Let's face it buying a Round is a pretty weird thing to do. After all, where else in life do you take it upon yourself to make an open-ended, unconditional commitment to pay for anything that other people - often complete strangers to you - might want? Do you walk into shoe-shops or furniture superstores and say "Right Who's having what?" No, you do not. And yet this is precisely what Pub Ethics requires you to do.

As a general rule this is alright and even if you don't come out even on any one visit, a long memory and a severe shortage of other friends will usually see you right in the end. Sometimes though, due to unforeseen financial problems or the fact you're drinking with people you don't really like, you might feel less inclined to follow the noble path. To do this properly and not get labelled a tight-wad for life it's important you learn How To Avoid Buying An Expensive Round.

1. Always offer to buy the first round. Though it sounds crazy, statistics prove that it's generally the cheapest. This doesn't apply if you're buying for ladies as they usually have a large Bailey's to start and then switch to Diet Coke.

2. Sit facing the door so you can see your drinking pals coming. This way you can neck down a bit of your pint and get them to buy you another before announcing you have to get back to set the timer on the video recorder.

3. If cornered with a large school of heavy hitters gradually introduce the topic of obesity and/or impaired sexual performance into the conversation. By the time your round comes, for some mysterious reason everyone will be on lime juice and soda.

4. Attempt to buy the last round. This requires sound timing so don't get too pissed first. Wait for the last orders bell to ring, begin a mid-length amusing anecdote, finish it then leap to your feet screaming "My Shout". By the time you actually get to the bar you should be late enough to ensure failure but not so late that everyone doesn't think you haven't tried. Works a treat every time.

THE IDEAL PUB

DART-BOARD - made of horse-hair so only the most determined and skilful arrows find their mark. Scoring should be by chalk-board only to encourage arithmetic skills

PUB FOOD - the same selection to be kept in large plastic dome until sold or universally declared unfit for human consumption. Selection to include at least one cornbeef sandwich, one shrunken scotch egg and two sausage rolls with mould on them.

NO MAN'S LAND - (SPACE BETWEEN CHAIRS AND BAR) - sacred space for harmless scrapping, dancing and acting out dramatic bits of long rambling stories

WOBBLY BROWN CIRCULAR TABLE - ideally this should be too small for more than one person to sit at or read a paper on in any comfort.

UNCOMFORTABLE STOOLS - chronic back-pain is the ideal climax to any half-decent night in the Pub and

BEER-MATS - a random selection spanning at least two decades. Though all of them should include entry to a big-prize competition that closed at least four years ago.

JUKEBOX - ideally this should be set at a volume that's not quite so loud you can enjoy the music but loud enough to muffle any conversation that does not include shouting. Music selection to include plenty of dreary 70's soul, Barry White, an unrepresentatively large amount of R.E.O. Speedwagon, four Irish rebel songs and scratched versions of 'Lady in Red' and 'I Just Called To Say I Love You'

SET OF LITTLE BRASS BELLS - balancing precariously on edge of picture rail.

POSTERS - included two faded shots of Norwegian fjords and advert for regional talent contest that never happened.

CLOCK - running at least 10 minutes fast so there's always time for one more extra pint.

BAR - either covered in ancient, foul-smelling beer mats or in ancient foul-smelling stains. In the real pub there should be little or no actual space to rest your pint in.

BABYCHAM STATUE - dust-covered and kept on a glass shelf behind the bar along with landlords bowling trophies and a framed photo of John F Kennedy.

REGULARS - to be greeted strictly on Nodding Terms Only though at Christmas and national holidays an additional "awright" is sometimes permitted.

HARP ICE BUCKET - filled mainly with cold water with faint traces of what looks suspiciously like fag ash.

CARPET - preferably marked with more cigarette burns than a sadomasochists convention.

'FUNNY' BAR NOTICES - including 'No Cheques Changed, Not Even Good Ones' & 'Do Not Ask For Credit As A Punch In The Kisser Often Offends'.

PRACTICAL JOKES

Practical jokes are insulting, childish and irritating... and therefore as essential to the art of Behaving Badly as wasps and a tartan rug are to a picnic. But like most anarchic forms, paradoxically the practical joke has a rigid set of rules:

- Don't be nice. If you want nice, do a funny monologue or some supposedly clever observational humour. Niceness never got the bucket of pigs' urine suspended over the door jam. Practical Jokes are meant to be cruel and pointlessly destructive. They are the Marquis de Sade, the Peter Lilley of the comedy world.

- Never intentionally maim anyone physically, even if it makes on paper for a very good PJ. Laughter and a trip in an ambulance with six inches of bone sticking out of your jeans make uneasy bedfellows.

- Never pull a practical joke on a girl you want to sleep with. It's a dignity thing. Beautiful women only go for blokes who have a sophisticated and witty sense of humour, or a flash car. So if you think sticking bangers up a frog's arse is hilarious, make sure you have at least a Ferrari Daytona.

- Target the successful and pompous. Tests carried out at the Government's Secret Research Centre at Aldermaston revealed that practical jokes were at their funniest when played on Harry Carpenter, the sports commentator, and Terence Conran, who used to run some shop or other.

- Be persistent, if a joke's worth doing once it's worth doing a hundred times. You won't believe how much funnier it gets when you see someone pissing into the clingfilm you've stretched across the loo for the fifth time in one week. On the other hand you may find this particular joke witless and irritating. It's a perspective thing.

TOP FIVE PRACTICAL JOKES

All these have been tried and tested by us in the last few months.

1. Fill in your flatmate's tax return for him, taking care to add plenty of noughts to the box marked 'Income From Rent'. For added fun you could either drop hints about off-shore accounts on the Isle of Sheppy or tuck a fiver into the envelope with a note asking the tax inspector to be a good boy like last year and have a drink on you.

2. Phone up your local radio station using a mate's full name and make a real dick of yourself on air. Answer all questions moronically, whoop loudly at the end of every word you say and burst into tears for no good reason when it's time to say goodbye. Make sure you say at least three things that are closely guarded secrets.

3. Sign your friend up for a home visit from the Mormons. Tell the speckie young Americans that you are a desperate if somewhat schizophrenic soul and that even if you deny them entry at first they are to be ruthlessly persistent with you till you give in.

4. By mistake let it slip to your flatmate or friend that you are throwing a surprise birthday party for them. Enjoy watching them pretend they don't know and then, at the last possible minute, cancel the party and go out, leaving them to spend their birthday alone.

5. Phone up your friend, pretending to be from another galaxy. Claim that he has been specially selected to further the human race by being put in a pod-shaped craft and sent out into space with a well-known Australian singer and former teen soap actress. This one won't work with everyone.

PARTIES

It goes without saying that Parties are the Elysian Fields of Behaving Badly in which you can romp to your heart's content making a genuine, five-star nuisance of yourself wherever you go. The problem is that they are also one of the few places where almost everyone is Behaving Badly in some way or another so you're going to have to be on your best form to stand out from the crowd.

GETTING INVITED

This is the hard part. It's more than likely your reputation for destructive and anti-social behaviour has preceeded you and potential Hosts greet the thought of putting your name on the guest list with all the enthusiasm of Michael Portillo turning up for a Gay Serviceman's convention. Come to think of it make that with <u>none</u> of the enthusiasm of Michael Portillo turning up for a Gay Serviceman's convention.

Still, this should not deter you.At the first sniff of the magic word 'Party', launch an immediate full-scale charm offensive on your potential host, wooing them with an irresistible mix of flowers, expensive gifts and thinly veiled threats. If that doesn't work then offer to drive your mates' van over to Calais to stock up on cheap booze and duty-free cream cheese dips. Hey presto - you're on the list. Of course then you'll actually have to go to France unless you take the sensible option and pull out with an unfortunate re-occurrence of your old RSI injury the night before you're due to go. Though your hosts will be suspicious, they can never actually prove your intentions were dishonourable - at least not unless they actually see you at the party using your injured hand to force the door off the fridge.

CRASHING

Crashing is always an option but it is really only any fun if:
a) you know absolutely NOBODY at the party you're busting into
b) it's a small family wedding/funeral
c) it's your own party

Otherwise leave it to the local psychos who know how to crash Parties with style and professionalism.

MAKING AN ENTRANCE

This is a much underestimated art in these informal times. Most people arrive at a party almost apologising for turning up in the first place, sheepishly waving their bottle of luke-warm Hungarian Chardonnay at their host like this might, just might, compensate for the campaign of wanton dullness they are about to wage in his living room. You, on the other hand, burst in through the door like a tidal wave clutching a single can of supermarket own brand lager and a half eaten kebab, grab the host or hostess and whirl them round the entrance hall like a long-lost relative. This is particularly effective if you haven't got the address wrong and knocked on an elderly neighbour's door by mistake.

ESTABLISHING YOUR TERRITORY

Like wars and games of American Football, Parties are mainly won or lost on the amount of territory you gain. A Bad Party experience will see you wandering around the place like a lost soul trying to break into conversations only to end up pretending to thumb through the books in a corner. A Good Party experience will see you setting up shop somewhere and making it the place where everyone else desperately wants to be. Only a scoundrel would try to achieve this by locking themselves into the toilet.

An ideal spot is the kitchen or if this isn't possible as near to the kitchen doorway as you can get without ending up spending your whole time passing things out to other guests. This is a prime pitch because:
a) You're close to the catering and can get your guzzling in before the goodies run out
b) People have to pass you to get another drink or fun-size sausage roll. This means you can effortlessly mingle and size up all the talent without looking for one moment as though you are. This is a Good Thing as nothing puts other guests off more than someone cruising around the place like a starving vulture round a carcass
c) You can make a quick and painless exit if you discover you're surrounded by a party full of Mortgage Brokers or worse still, unfanciable women. Mind you, if you hang around long enough and drink your way through the entire contents of the fridge you'll soon put the last thing right

SMALL TALK

People worry far too much about the quality of their Small Talk. The simple solution is not to make any. Instead, either simply put on a pair of dark glasses, stand to one side with an ironic grin and let other people make the conversational running (the so-called Art Student strategy) or take a true Badly Behaved route and make nothing but Big Talk. This involves looking a chic (never a Bloke - Big Talk is wasted on other Blokes) straight in the eye and coming out with the most direct and challenging remark that your addled brain can come up with, ie:
a) So. Will you marry me?
b) Erm...

Maybe Big Talk is more difficult than we first thought.

FOOD AND DRINK

Drink your own and do your best not to heave over the living room curtains. Simple rules but easily forgotten in the heat of battle.

DANCING

If carpet was meant to be danced on how come you never see a nice polyester Axeminster in night-clubs? The simple truth is that EVERYBODY LOOKS A PRAT DANCING ON CARPET which means that when the sad and tragic gyrating to crap hits of the 80's starts you can either;
a) refuse to come out of the kitchen on aesthetic grounds
b) leap in and make a tosser of yourself like everyone else with total impunity

Conversely, you may find that Carpet Effect cancels out any rhythmic and co-ordinational disadvantages you might have and that you're actually easily the best dancer there. If this is the case try not to blow it by either starting a conga or making repeated requests for the person in charge of the music to play anything by Whitesnake.

PARTY SEX

Now we're getting to the heart of the matter. The thought of playing a quick and totally unexpected game of Trains and Tunnels is, after all, the only thing that makes the whole ridiculous charade even vaguely tolerable. Outside of teenage birthday parties and gatherings involving junior members of the Royal Family, actually achieving it in situ is altogether another matter.

1. Timing is everything. Leave it too late and you'll either be too pissed to raise anything other than the toilet seat or all the bedrooms will be chock full of guests who got their act together while you were still pretending to be interested in where she went for her holidays. On the other hand if you go for it too early you'll only end up with everyone's coats being thrown all over you.

2. Ladies sometimes have this weird reluctance to move in a matter of minutes from polite conversation about the host's interior furnishings to going at it like dogs in a dark spot at the bottom of the garden. Overcome this hurdle by pretending that you live there and that it's perfectly OK to do that on your duvet. This move might not work quite so well if your potential bed-partner is also the Hostess.

3. Be cheeky. If you wait till the party's over and try the old Let's Share A Cab Home routine you may well end up spending the implausibly long trip back sitting in the front while she sits in the back trying to make it up to her boyfriend.

4. Don't be too fussy. It's hard enough getting to even talk to the good-looking ones without trying to take them roughly from behind in a complete stranger's airing cupboard. That said it doesn't mean for one moment you shouldn't ask...

MAKING YOUR EXIT

Oh yes. Sadly at some time or other even the best parties have to end and unless you really want to be still there when the neighbours come round you're gonna have to make your exit. Like your entrance this should be accomplished with style and flair. Don't hang around all night waiting for a mini-cab. Just put your clothes on, wipe as many of the stains off your trousers as the tasteful throw on the settee can handle and get the fuck out of there a.s.a.p. before they discover what really happened to that large dish of home-made humus.

After all, when all's said and done, you'd like to be invited back next time, wouldn't you?

For further advice on Special Party situations see OFFICE PARTIES, FUN AT FUNERALS and SERIOUSLY PISSING OFF YOUR RELATIVES.

PULLING

Pulling is a subject of such overwhelming importance that any one entry can only ever scratch the surface of it. After all , isn't everything we do in life - with the exception of going to footie matches and phoning up your Mum - in some way connected to the goal of closing the gap between your lips and someone else's?

That said there are a few general remarks we can make:

1. Pulling chics isn't easy.   In fact scientific studies have shown that in these sexually confused days Pulling is the third most terrifying thing any man can do after chucking girlfriends and bringing overdue books back to theLibrary.   Don't let this get to you though.   Make your fear your friend.   Or if you can't do that at least make it someone you nod to when you see them in the local newsagent.

2. If approached in the proper state of mind Pulling can be one of the great Participation sports and as such the usual sporting rules apply:

a) Practise makes perfect.   If you blow one big fixture then try and arrange an easier friendly as soon as possible afterwards.   No one should expect to put the ball in the net with a screaming 30 yard drive every time.

b) Don't get too bogged down in tactics.   Play your natural game and let the ball do the work.

c) Remember that it's never over till it's over and any-one can come back from being three nil down to clinch an unlikely victory in extra time.

d) Try not to drink too much before a big game.   It effects your stamina, your timing goes and throwing up on the opposition tends to mar the match for both sides

3. Ohcose your Pulling Place wisely.   Though it may seem like a good idea to concentrate on fun pubs and night-clubs they're usually packed to the rafters with other blokes doing the same thing with more money and less of a sense of irony.   Instead try Pulling at art galleries, theatre bars, political demonstrations, cash point machines, traffic jams and any major tourist attraction that bus-loads of foreign language students might go to.

4. Don't let Pulling be a chore.   Keep yourself inter-ested by constantly inventing a whole new identity for yourself each and every time you try to Pull. For some strange reason women really do respond more positively to you as Racing Driver Who Threw the World Championship Away For The Love Of A Woman Who Then Died in Childbirth than they do to you as Trainee Marketing Manager From Swindon With Money Worries. If caught out in a lie DO NOT PANIC.   Just laugh sweetly, congratulate her on her astuteness and launch straight in with another set of completely unnecessary fictions.

PULLING

Nurses

Why:
Haven't you seen any old 'Carry On' and 'Doctor...' films? Everybody fancies Nurses. They are selfless, hard-working dedicated servants of humanity without whom the fabric of society would crumble into dust. And, of course, traditionally they go like trains.

When/Where:
Hospitals or bowling alleys where groups of trainee nurses always go to relax after a hard day saving lives and being rude to patients' relatives.

What not to wear:
Large bandages, casts, Bupa stickers or anything that makes you look like a hospital administrator.

What to say:
"Yes but I think you need someone to take care of you"

What not to say:
"You do all that for £20 a day. Christ, you must be desperate"

Degree of permitted sexual explicitness:
5/5 - but only if you use the medical terms.

Danger Factor:
1 - Nurses are used to being Pulled and treat it as part of the job. The only people who perhaps should not try this are men in hospital to watch their wives giving birth.

Your Best Mate's Girlfriend

Why:
Well, you've got to haven't you?

When/Where:
Choose a moment when your mate is out of town on a business trip or fishing holiday. Pop round to check if she's Ok not forgetting to bring three bottles of wine and a ten pack of Continental & Coloureds with you. Work on her insecurities, pour wine down her neck and make love on the living room floor.

What not to wear:
Anything belonging to your mate - shirt, jumper etc.

What to say:
"I know both of us feel bad about letting Terry down but isn't it an even worse crime to let yourself down?"

What not to say:
"Tell you what. Old Tel was right. You are a screamer"

Degree of permitted sexual explicitness:
4/5 - but only when you're on to the third bottle.

Danger Factor:
2 - if it all goes wrong you pretend you were only testing her for his sake. If it all goes right then wey-hey! She's got even more to lose than you by it coming out.

Your Girlfriend's Mother

Why:
Girls are like colour photocopies of their Mothers.
Why not have the original?
When/Where:
Away from the family home.   Wait till she pops up
for an extended visit, pay her lots of attention
and then, when your bird's not paying attention
whip her Mum off out for a quick look round the
shops and go for it.
What not to wear:
Anthing your girlfriend has made for you or given
you in front of the entire family at Christmas.
What to say:
"You know Jean at first I thought I fancied you
because you look so like Carol.   Now I know it's
the other way round"
What not to say:
"I wonder if Carol's dislike of oral sex is genetic?"
Degree of permitted sexual explicitness:
9 - even if they pretend otherwise Mothers love
smutty talk, especially if you can come out with it
when they're baking.
Danger Factor:
10 - though most Mothers like their daughter's
boyfriend to flirt with them very few expect him
to leap on them in the kitchen and stick his
tongue down their ear.   This is especially
true if they're happily married for thirty-four
years and have never slept with anyone other than
their husbands.   Still, it's a challenge...

Actresses

No sane man in his right mind should EVER attempt
to go out with an actress.

Advanced Pulling

Policewomen

Why:
There really is something about a chic in a uniform,
especially when it's her own.   Maybe it's the power,
maybe it's the challenge, maybe it's because they're
the one group of ladies the Darrens never go for.
Play your cards right and you should have a pretty
clear run.
When/Where:
Opportunities abound.   Generally easier if you're
a victim of crime rather than a criminal as it's
pretty hard to get much Pulling done when her mates
are kicking seven kinds of shite out of you in the
back of a meat-wagon.
What not to wear:
Hooded tops, football shirts, any Tee-shirt that has
the word 'Fuck' printed on it.
What to say:
"It must be immensely difficult keeping the streets
safe in an amoral and divided society"
What not to say:
"Wanna share a spliff?"
Degree of permitted sexual explicitness:
2/5 (on duty) 5/5 (off)
Danger Factor:
8/10.   She's more than likely married to a psycho-
pathic Policeman.

QUESTIONNAIRE

IS IT LOVE OR LUST WITH YOUR GIRLFRIEND

Going out with a girl is like entering a new town. Either you get lucky and go straight through onto the next or you get unlucky and end up on the ring-road heading for the industrial estate. In this case you need to know exactly where you are. Is it Love or Lust? Is it time to slow down or slip into fifth and head for the hills? Find out with our simple but effective quiz.

1. How did you feel when you first met your girl?

a) You had butterflies in your tummy and and your heart went squidgy.

b) You didn't fancy her but still reckoned that talking to her was better than listening to your mate's thesis on 'Why United should never have let Hughsie go'?.

c) Now when <u>did</u> I meet my girl?

2. Which statement most closely represents how you feel about her?

a) You can't get her out of your mind and you think Barnaby is a great name for a boy.

b) You like her when she comes round – preferably with a bag of shopping in each hand.

c) Well...you can't pull your pud every night, can you?

3. When she talks about sex with her last bloke, what's your reaction?

a) You see red with jealousy and start breaking things (of hers)

b) Curious but slightly scared to find out more in case he was bigger and better than you.

c) She shouldn't say nasty things about your best mate.

4. What impresses you most about her?

a) The way she slurps her soup and sucks her spaghetti and still maintains her femininity.

b) The way she drinks pints and always buys a round

c) Her tits and arse.

5. What do you do when her girlfriend keeps coming round?

a) Make her a pot of tea and quiz her for amusing anecdotes about their school-days.

b) You tolerate her as long as she flirts with you and laughs at all your jokes.

c) You spend the entire time fantasising about a threesome.

6. What do you do when she's away?

a) Every day is a torture to you. You ring her answer phone constantly just so you can hear her voice.
b) You feel like you've been released on parole. You start phoning people you fancy but couldn't normally get away with seeing.
c) Rent her underwear out to all your friends and panic when none of them bring it back.

7. What's the best thing about arguments with your girlfriend?

a) We never argue.
b) It's a good excuse to storm off to the pub with your mates and get trolleyed.
c) It's nice to see a grown woman cry.

8. How do you see your relationship in ten year's time?

a) Engaged and going to furniture shops.
b) Split up, although you occasionally fantasise about getting your leg over for old time's sake.
c) You'll see her in the street and find you've totally forgotten her name.

HOW DID YOU SCORE?

Mostly "C"s

Any deviation from this and you should chuck her immediately. the sound principle of - if you're happy, she's happy. Nice one. You're in a good, healthy relationship based on

Mostly "B"s

spare room. Get out now or live to regret it. brides-maids dresses and babyish pastel colours for the of fun, a harmless fling. She's choosing colour schemes for You're in the danger-zone pal. You think it's just a bit

Mostly "A"s

take it in turns to put the rubbish out. by the Volvo-load. If you don't want the romance to fade, Yup, you've got it bad. Settling down, marriage and babies

We could take football or leave it - until it emerged recently as the sport of mad-arse behaviour both on and off the pitch. Just to show how far the game has come, here are 10 examples of how Roy of the Rovers would have to adapt to today's standards of soccer Bad Behaviour:

1. Roy's clean-cut image is dented when he stars in a TV advert in which he is required to slap a 10-year-old child about a bit and steal his pork scratchings.

2. Roy accepts a bribe from a shady Indonesian businessman to ensure that Melchester Rovers go down in the first round. Feigning amnesia brought on by a tampered-with quarter of orange at half time, he picks up the ball at the half-way mark, rounds his own team and buries it in the net, shrieking "Roy! I am Roy!"

3. Roy incurs criticism and ridicule when he crops his legend-ary hair and dyes it blond. He explains to the press: "Oh, fuck off and leave me alone."

4. After being sent off for repeatedly calling the referee 'Maureen', Roy is angered by abuse from the crowd. Using his legendary spring-heels, he leaps in among spectators and bites the nose of 24 year-old Dale Thug. He is sentenced to 100 hours of community service, teaching ball skills to Melchester's growing number of homeless people.

5. After winning a 'Yard of Malibu' contest in a night-club on the way home Roy roughs up a taxi driver for refusing to carry him upstairs to bed.

6. Roy accepts a 'bung' from Stig Stigsson, a Scandinavian soccer fixer, Roy explains that he thought 'bung' was Scandi-navian for 'mug of Bovril' so had accepted with his legendary alacrity.

7. Roy bursts into tears when a booking renders him ineligible for Melchester's FA Cup final appearance. He pulls himself together when told that weeping is now old hat.

8. After a long lay-off, most of it spent mooching around Man-chester jazz clubs with Eric Cantona's French Dada-ist set, Roy's hitherto solid grasp of language deserts him. At a press conference, Roy argues passionately that "the anchovies that lie limply on the seafood pizza of time shall doo-be-doo-be-doo all the way home."

9. Roy head-butts the opposition goalkeeper for "staring at me". He is sent to prison for three months.

10. On his release, Roy checks himself into one of Melchester's five drying-out clinics. At another tearful press conference, to illustrate how much help he needs Roy uses a tube from the legendary "Roy of the Rovers Blow-Football Game" to snort several grams of a white powder, which turns out to be his manager's dandruff, an act of cannibalism which disgusts all those present.

RADIO PHONE-INS

For Blokes who, for some unknown reason, aren't pulling back the duvet every night to find Michelle Pfeiffer waiting for them in her silkiest nightie, Late-Night Radio Phone-ins are a true godsend. Just imagine: for the price of a local phone call you can spend your last waking minutes annoying the hell out of hundreds, even thousands of complete strangers with a potent mix of dubious logic and interminable anecdotes - and you don't even have to put your trousers on to do it.

Phone-In Rules

- Always use a made-up name and location. If in doubt call yourself Reg from Hounslow, except if your name really is Reg and you live in a vibrant West London suburb not far from Heathrow Airport when you should probably think of something else.

- Don't crawl to the presenter, greet them like a long-lost friend or agree with everything they say. Instead try to sound as much as possible like a normal Phone-in caller. This is what nutters and cab drivers do. Instead try to sound as much as possible like a normal Phone-in caller.
a) Clear your throat several times as though you were about to make a speech that will change the fate of nations.
b) Say the word 'Yes' as though you had already said something interesting and important.
c) Launch into your mad and bigoted tirade against nylon socks.

- Don't use any words or phrases that are part of your everyday vocabulary. It's a fact of life that <u>everyone</u> on phone-ins sounds like a policeman giving evidence so sprinkle your speech with plenty of "appertainings", "aforementioneds", and "I'm not racist but"s. Don't take the policeman parallel too far though as pointless sneering sarcasm doesn't come over too well on the radio.

- Whatever you do don't allow the presenter to cut you off in mid flow. Instead when you feel the ending coming bring your speech to as large and hysterical a climax as you can muster, throw in a wild and unsubstantiated sexual allegation against a member of the cabinet, shout 'God Save The Queen' and hang up. Before you know it you'll be a Phone-in star and they'll be gagging for you to come back.

RECYCLING

Though it might at first sound like a conflict of interests, the bloke who wants to behave Badly ignores Environmental concerns at his peril - as lots of birds really go for blokes who seem all soft and caring and worried about the future of the planet. Just be sure not to let your guard slip and reply, when they ask if you want to go clubbing: "Yeah, 'cause I really hate all those soppy-looking baby seals." This will not go down well.

EMPTY PLASTIC 2 LITRE CIDER OR LAGER BOTTLES

UNUSED "ARIELETTE"

HANDY "NOVELTY INDOORS SKITTLES SET"

"BISTRO-STYLE SINGLE STEM VASE"

For that Tapas-bar chic look.

ORDINARY BROWN OR GREEN GLASS LAGER BOTTLE

AMSTEL BIER

True "Bad Behaviour" is, however, supremely eco-friendly as it typically accompanies a domestic lifestyle low in its usage of such potentially planet-threatening chemicals as washing-up liquid, bleach, soap powder, toilet cleaner, etc., etc., and damaging aerosoles like furniture polish and air-freshener.

Thats why we have developed our own unique "Bad Behaviour Gift Range" which cleverly recycles the commonest items of household waste - lager bottles, beer cans, and fag packets - by turning them into enchanting yet thoroughly practcal gift items.

FRIES PACKET

FOIL FAST FOOD TRAY

MILK SHAKE CUP

FUN "FIFTIES RETRO" DESK SET

FOUR
EMPTY
BEER CANS,
STILL JOINED
BY PLASTIC
← YOKE

"4-HOLE
 SINK TIDY"
(In rust-proof Aluminium)

BENT OVER
INTERLINKED
RING PULLS

BEER →
CAN

(CLOSE-UP
TO SHOW HOW
RING PULLS
ARE LINKED)

BUD

Interestingly, "Necessity being
the Single-Mother of Invention"
the following charmingly-folksy
gift items were all originally
developed as last-minute presents
for girlfriends whose birthdays
we had somehow overlooked.
We didn't spend all those years
watching "Blue Peter" simply in
the hope of seeing Sarah Greene
trampolining in a leotard, or
Caron Keating snorkelling in a
one-piece swimming-cozzy. Janet
Ellis in jodhpurs was also
something of a bonus.

EMPTY FAG PACKETS
STUCK ON A BIT OF WOOD
WITH NAMES WRITTEN
ON THEM IN FELT TIP
↓

SAGE | THYME | ROSE MARY | BASIL

"SPICE-RACK TO HOLD
SPICE JAR REFILLS"

NOVELTY
LOO CHAIN
AND PULL
"The can for
the can"

SOFA

Love your sofa - you spend many hours on it, it is your friend.
It has received unto it for God's sake your most intimate juices
and your girlfriends' most intimate juices while still in the
we-have-to-do-it-now stage of your relationship, as distinct
from the I'm-not-doing-it-unless-you-take-the-rubbish-out stage.
Your sofa - or 'Tammy' as we sometimes call her - has cheer-
fully welcomed into her interior the twin heats of you and
your girlfriends' bottoms.   It's got chunks of your pizza in
it.   A perfectly drinkable combination of lager and Cuppasoup
can be had by gently sucking the cushioned areas.   Your spit
has rained down upon it as you excitedly explained to someone
how you saw Zsa Zsa Gabor on the bus, or someone very like
her.   You know more about that sofa than you do about your
parents.

There are three basic sofa situations (or, if you like,
sofituations):

- You and another bloke drinking lager while
watching the TV

- You and your special lady intertwined like
Bacchic sex gods while watching the TV

- You on your own on the sofa shouting through
to your special lady in the kitchen to keep the
noise down while she's cooking because you're
watching the TV.

You will have already enjoyed those, now try the following:

- Attempt the Most Mates On A Sofa record, currently held by Dave Miles and 41 mates on the sofa in his Northampton squat during a party in 1986. Dave's brother-in-law cracked a rib so do be careful.

- Estimate the number of hours per week you spend on the sofa, subtract by your age, divide by the number of times you have had sex on it. Write the number down. Throw it away.

- Surfing. Put on Beach Boys CD, mount sofa, stand with arms out in surfing position. It's safe, it's cheap, it's dry and you don't have to go to Cornwall. Advanced sofa-surfers (or, if you like, sofers) can recreate 'the tube' with sofa cushions and newspapers

- Lie on the floor, paralled with the sofa. This is apparently what it was like to sleep next to the late, great 'Mama' Cass.

- Beat the back of the sofa vigorously. In the resultant dust storm, recreate battles from the North Africa campaign in the crucial early stages of World War 11.

SIMULATED ORGASM

Bad behaviour from girlfriends is normally a pretty tepid affair as though - bless them - their heart isn't really in it (although see Dumping, Unceremonial). But they have been known to commit one act so monstrous it makes a little bit of horseplay with an inflated condom and your neighbour's tortoise look like very small potatoes indeed - WHEN YOUR GIRLFRIEND SIMULATES AN ORGASM. Most men say it's never happened to them. In fact that's what we say. But it's happened to these blokes we met once and they were so shaken up by it that we want to talk about it in our book - in question and answer form to make it look like a posh medical publication rather than a tawdry cash-in comedy book aimed squarely at the Christmas market.

How can I tell a real orgasm from a simulated one?
If it's real the chest area and face will become redder, the vagina will contract several times, and a few minutes later she'll be propped up on her elbow in bed urging you to talk about your feelings. If it's simulated, the chest area will keep it's bored, alabaster white, the mouth will dilate several times into huge yawns and she'll do some wooden groaning culminating in a rather lacklustre beep. Minutes later she'll be asleep or tapping off with a swarthy waiter on the night bus home.
Girls - blokes know. We've seen Julian Sands in Arachnaphobia. We know bad acting when we see it.

Goddammit it's happened. What should I do?
The first time you persuade yourself that you don't mind. You hear yourself saying "She's been under a lot of stress lately, what with her boss Peter still not respecting her as a person and all." You could pretend you didn't notice, or that you enjoyed it as a kind of empty ritual. Better to bring the conversation round to Meg Ryan in When Harry Met Sally and say darkly "You could tell she was pretending because she didn't do that thing that tells every guy it was genuine." If she carries on doing it after that, dump her and find yourself a girl who can't even be tapped on the shoulder without grabbing you and gasping "That was incredible".

Should I blame myself in any way?
Maybe you shouldn't be reading this book.

Should I fake it myself to get my own back?
No. Why should you. You deserve to ejaculate. If though
you've had a massive overdose of lager and suddenly realise
you're in an 'unable to finish what you've started' situation, the best way to fake a male orgasm is to go silent,
shudder a bit, say "Thanks" and immediately roll over and go
to sleep. That convinces them.

Why do they do it?

Because they misguidedly believe we prefer the Unreal Thing
to nothing at all. On the contrary, most guys consider the
female climax like a White Christmas - it's nice if it happens
but you don't stand there waiting at the top of the hill with
your sledge just in case.

When is simulated ecstasy completely okay?
When it's on a pop record. Donna Summer knew a thing or two
when, in her 1976 single, she insisted she wanted to Love To
Love You Baby and we believed her. For most men, hearing the
record was an immediate out-of-pants experience. White adol-
escents roamed the streets looking hungrily for a black chick.
Donna was preceded by the more stately Je t'aime... moi non
plus, sung by Jane Birkin and the extraordinarily aptly-named
Serge. Since then we've had various disco hits with gasps and
groans and they've all been well worth buying, frankly.

STAG NIGHTS

Stag Nights are the Test Matches of the Bad Behaviour sporting calender and as such should be taken as seriously and prefer- ably last as long as any five-day event at Lords.

In olden times Stag Nights were designed to humiliate the Groom and punish him for having the cheek to abandon his life of drunken debauchery for the promise of regular sex with his young wife. Though times have changed in lots of other ways this is still true. REMEMBER. If the Groom doesn't end the event bruised, naked and tearfully swearing he never wants to see any of you again you may as well not have bothered having a Stag do in the first place.

Stag Nights have a very set formula and whatever your position is in the Wedding To Be hierarchy you have a set role which you must play without variation.

THE GROOM: You are the sacrificial victim. You spend the whole time smiling a lot while panicking inside about what terrible thing is about to happen to you. Of course you must drink EVERYTHING that's put into your hands even if it's still alive and moving around rather threateningly at the bottom of the glass. When it comes to the Strippergram time you must grin, make a big show of being unwilling to let her take off all your clothes and smear whipped cream all over your marital jewels. In the event that she is a heavy duty Stippergram who's prepared to take it all the way you must do your best not to let the lads down by totally failing to produce anything that even faintly resembles a hard-on. But remember, nobody but nobody wants to see their mate having it away in front of them and though they may stamp and roar their approval they're all secretly hating you inside.

THE BEST MAN: As organiser and tormentor in chief you are the most important man on the Stag Night and you're quite within your rights to let everyone else know this by keeping the next stage in the proceedings secret and making all the foot soldiers buy you drinks as well. Your prime task task is to keep the Groom within arms reach except when he's off in the Gents chucking up when the etiquette is to keep at least two brick walls between you. Whatever your particular circumstances are The Best Man is honour-bound to try to get off with the Strippergram. This is best attempted before you've paid her as, unless she's one of your immediate family, they normally don't hang around much afterwards.

THE MATE: As a normal run of the mill mate at a Stag Night you have the simple but vital role in proceedings, namely getting off your face as quickly as possible and laughing at the Best Man's jokes, however terrible they are. As a Mate one of your main tasks is to cause as much noise and mayhem as possible to steal the Groom's thunder other than the devastatingly witty piss taking remarks required of you by the rule of Stag. You are, of course, quite at liberty to take any of your clothes off in sympathy with The Groom, though you musn't do this within three feet of the Strippergram or the Best Man will pull out his red card and send you home.

THE MATE'S MATE: An apparently difficult role as you are usually someone who's just been brought along for the ride to make up the numbers and convince the Groom that he's popular. Having no stake in the event or real right to be there you are, on the other hand, usually the one who has the best time and/or discovers you went to school with the Strippergram and get off with her in the car-park. Unless you're so anonymous you get left behind at the first pub you generally can't lose in this role.

STAG NIGHT RULES
Never EVER tell either your own or other people's girlfriends anything about what actually happened on a Stag Night as this inevitably leads to arguments and/or the cancellation of the wedding.

Arrive early and stay as late as humanly possible. Any attempt to make an early exit on the grounds of catching the last bus will lead to you getting a good kicking. And quite right too.

Don't be a tight-wad. Serious Stagging isn't ever done on the cheap and you should be prepared to blow at least half a month's wages on one night of untrammelled drinking and hideously expensive Greek food. If you're really skint bring a flusher friend with you as your Mate's Mate and every time a round comes up push him up to the bar with the cry of "Has everyone met my mate Chris?".

NB
Apparently there's a hotel somewhere in the Sussex countryside which only caters for Stag Parties. There's a help-yourself bar that's open 24 hours a day, a plastic-covered dining-room so you can chuck food at each other at dinner time, five different porn channels and loads of gorgeous Swedish waitresses who come down at night and sleep with all the guests. On the otherhand one of us probably only heard about it in a dream.

The first time you go shopping with your girlfriend (for clothes and shoes, it's always clothes and shoes) you are attentive and interested, muttering comments like "Yes, the blue definitely brings out your steely qualities without suggesting in any way a wintry person" and "Back into Dolcis, great!". The second time you start to bring a touch of realism to the party: "No, I don't think it makes your arse look like a big arse, but... whatever", "Dolcis again - what happened to one-stop shopping?" By the third time you go shopping together, and for the rest of your relationship, you become a throbbing beacon of frustration and find yourself shouting in the middle of Miss Selfridge "Pink, green, orange, do you think I honestly give a toss?" and "I'd rather insert my penis into my Russell Hobbs long-slot toaster than go into Dolcis again".

There are bonuses, though. The air in and around the changing area in women's clothes shops is heavy with sexual promise. Behind that thin curtain (which, like an Italian teenager, never quite goes all the way) they've only got their pants on. Erotic phrases drift out, like "I'll have to take my bra off - God that's better" and "It rides up when I bend over, look."

If there are individual changing rooms your girlfriend might invite you into the cubicle. It's cramped, there are two blood-stained Band-Aids in the corner, the carpet looks like someone's had a barbecue on it and there's an odour, but if you're lucky it's a thrilling odour, a mixture of perfume and warm woman. You have two choices: you try to get out as quickly as possible by telling her the clothes make her look as arousing as Kylie and Wynona Ryder exploring their sexuality together in a Beverly Hills jacuzzi, or you attempt to join the clothes-shop equivalent of the Mile-High Club: the No-More-Than-Two-Items-in-The-Cubicle Club.

If she doesn't invite you into the cubicle, you will have to pass the hours you spend in the shop by

- holding various clothes up against your body, the girls' way, swishing this way and that and saying "I'd have to buy xsome new shoes to go with this" in a really whiney way

- pretending you have a nosebleed. Girls don't get nosebleeds and are almost as scared of them as they are of wasps

- doing your own racing-style commentary on proceedings: "And Belly-button top is leading, the favourite Belly-button top, Belly - oh it's refused! White Strappy thing has taken over, White Strappy Th-, no - that's gone too. Sensible Jacket now has the lead, no! would you believe it, it's run out! Sensible Jacket has run out...!"

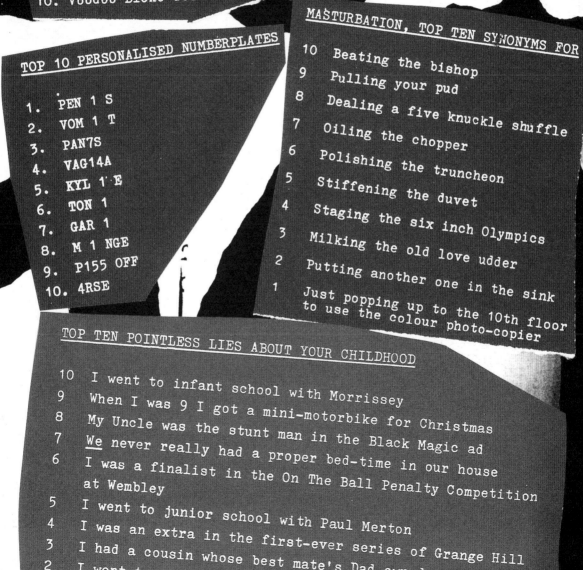

TOP 10 ITEMS IN BLOKES' BATHROOM CUPBOARDS

1. Horn aftershave
2. Lager Devil shaving mousse
3. Guy! shampoo.
4. Comanche Babe hair gel
5. Michael Winner Range spot cream
6. Bastard skin toner
7. Resolve
8. Testosterone Bully hair conditioner
9. Gary Linekar Foot Balm
10. Voodoo Bloke deodorant

OP TENS

TOP 10 PERSONALISED NUMBERPLATES

1. PEN 1 S
2. VOM 1 T
3. PAN7S
4. VAG14A
5. KYL 1 E
6. TON 1
7. GAR 1
8. M 1 NGE
9. P155 OFF
10. 4RSE

MASTURBATION, TOP TEN SYNONYMS FOR

10. Beating the bishop
9. Pulling your pud
8. Dealing a five knuckle shuffle
7. Oiling the chopper
6. Polishing the truncheon
5. Stiffening the duvet
4. Staging the six inch Olympics
3. Milking the old love udder
2. Putting another one in the sink
1. Just popping up to the 10th floor to use the colour photo-copier

TOP TEN POINTLESS LIES ABOUT YOUR CHILDHOOD

10. I went to infant school with Morrissey
9. When I was 9 I got a mini-motorbike for Christmas
8. My Uncle was the stunt man in the Black Magic ad
7. We never really had a proper bed-time in our house
6. I was a finalist in the On The Ball Penalty Competition at Wembley
5. I went to junior school with Paul Merton
4. I was an extra in the first-ever series of Grange Hill
3. I had a cousin whose best mate's Dad owned a porn shop
2. I went to senior school with Suggs
1. Anything at all to do with your first sexual experiences, obviously

DOWN IT IN ONE

SILICONE BOUNCY CASTLE

KYLIE ROLLER COASTER

PICK OF THE DAY

● **E.R. CHANNEL 4, 10.00pm.**

Soppy American hospital drama much watched by girlies and loved for its authenticity (ie contrived soapy plots). Of course, the real reason they tune in like vultures on Wednesday nights is to see a wide range of people having their stomachs ripped apart by a caring psychopath with small round glasses. There are two main reasons why chics love the show: 1; they like seeing male patients die; that's one less of the bastards to worry about; 2; they like seeing women patients get horribly mutilated. This is especially true if they are good-looking and have a baby on the way. Of course in both cases girlies pretend they really care about the individual's human tragedy but we know their tears are tears of joy. Most sensible lads are in the pub at 10 o'clock on a Wednesday night but if you are forced to watch it don't worry. Unlike in Casualty, in E.R. at least all the nurses and lady doctors don't look like they've just been wheeled out on a trolley from the morgue.

TELEVISION CHOICE

● **WORLD IN ACTION , ITV, 8.30pm.**

We don't usually watch documentaries unless they're about how Tyneside housewives are having to turn to stripping to survive or about how British strippers are earning fortunes by going to Germany to strip there. But this one tonight isn't about stripping, so it'll be quite a departure for us. It's about the scandal of how students are being forced to take jobs in topless bars just to make ends meet, as it were, what with their grants being so small these days. We see them going about their horrible jobs, pulling pints in the semi-nude, looking miserable and wishing they were sitting at home in their duffel coats with their head inside an enormous text book. Good to see a documentary taking a few risks and not afraid to show just how sleazy life can get. Um. So that's what it's about.

TOTTY RATING

(T) Good

(TT) V.Good

(TTT) Excellent

(TTTT) Incredible

BBC 1

7.00 TOP OF THE POPS (T): Totally unmissable, especially now the audience as well as the acts are all dressed in short skirts and little tops that reveal their belly-buttons. Presented by some bloke who thinks he's funny.

7.30 EASTENDERS (T): Bianca wants to help Ruth but only ends up pissing off Ricky who wants to help Sam who's pissed off with Grant for helping Phil piss off Pauline. Or something like that. Maybe Sam will wear her cut-down jeans again.

8.00 HOW DO THEY DO THAT: More miracles with Des and his tiny friend. Take notes and re-cycle to fill in those awkward gaps in the pub. Would be even better if Des had a real babe to letch over.

8.30 MEN OF THE WORLD: totally unrealistic sit-com about two blokes who spend their whole lives talking bollocks and trying to get off with women. Don't they realise both these are deadly serious activities? Worse still, one of the blokes has got a dodgy perm.

9.00 NEWS: weather: not worth watching - too depressing. All the decent looking weathergirls are on ITV.

9.30 CHANDLER & CO: Drama series about a candle-making company.

10.30 MATCH OF THE SEVENTIES: oodles of tasty footy action from the days when men were men and girls didn't even pretend to be interested in 22 blokes chasing a ball around muddy field. Great names, great burns. An absolute must, like your Esso medal collection in 3D.

11.30 FILM: Castaway (TTT). Fascinating story of beautiful young girl and older man who decide to live together on a desert island. Ollie Reid is on top form as a randy drunken goat being tortured by Amanda Donahoe's unreasonable refusal to sleep with him. A great story, beautifully shot and acted. And Amanda obligingly spends most of the film with her top off. Challenging stuff.

1.10 NEWS AND WEATHER: followed by Close down.

1.25 DOCTOR'S PROGRAMMES: scrambled so unwatchable unless you're off your face on a lager and Benylin cocktail when, strangely enough they become completely comprehensible.

BBC 2	CH 4	ITV

BBC 2

7.30 BIG SCIENCE: Something about lizards.

8.00 READY STEADY COOK: About cooking, or another programme about Roger Cook sprinting after bent timeshare salesmen and getting shot at.

8.30 TOP GEAR: About cars. Gets good viewing figures because about a million people think it's about where to score really excellent drugs and another million think it's about clothes, albeit with a strong motoring bias.

9.00 FILM: Room with a View (TT): Helena Bonham Carter experiences a sexual awakening and as a result so do we all. Spoilt by the scene when the blokes run round the pond naked, an example of exploitative filmmaking at its worst.

10.30 NEWSNIGHT (T): Has Bosnia Got a Future? No idea what this about. If you're lucky you might get Kirsty Wark presenting.

11.15-2.30 OPEN UNIVERSITY: Education show. It's all too easy to take the piss out of the presenters.

CH 4

6.00 BLOSSOM (TT): More tales of heart-ache as a sassy young girl makes that difficult and painful journey into womanhood and tries to avoid her Dad's wandering hands. The question is; has Blossom actually done it yet and if not why not? She's a good looking girl. She dances, she sings. Oh boy yes, she dances...

6.30 ROSEANNE (T): Women's comedy. Two fat Americans get even fatter and slag off their ugly children. Yuk.

7.00 CHANNEL FOUR NEWS: even longer and more boring than the rest.

7.50 THE SLOT: great title, shame about the programme. Lots of people moaning about things.

8.00 BROOKSIDE: who cares now the fit lessie's dead?

8.30 PREDATORS (T): Seals. Nature programme presented by Gaby Roslin. Half an hour of total joy in the company of a doe-eyed, elegant creature with the most strokable skin on earth. The seals aren't bad either.

9.00 ELLEN (TT): Totally unrealistic comedy about a gorgeous American blond with blue eyes who week in week out can never get a shag. Impossible, even with American men. Still worth sticking with for research purposes and the bit part actresses.

9.30 FRIENDS (TTTT): Now this is funny. Three blokes, three girls. They all live opposite each other and have keys to each other's flats. They flirt, they chat, they get jealous when anybody goes out with anyone else. Only one thing is slightly untrue to life.

The boys never even try to get a snog in nor do their eyes follow the girl's bottoms whenever they walk across the room. The girls also laugh at the guys' jokes too much. Modern women never find Blokes funny,

10.00 E.R. (T): (see pick of the day)

11.05 FILM; DROWNING BY NUMBERS: Incomprehensible arthouse movie set in Norfolk. There's lots of nudity though involving Juliet Stevenson and Joely Richardson so might be worth sticking with,

12.30 UNITED STATES OF TELEVISION (TT): Compilation show of all the most shocking bits from US cable shows. Unmissable combination of smut and bumbling amateurism. Expect the real filth to come in flashframes so video if you can.

1.25 THE BEST OF THE BEST OF THE WORD (T): See your day out with Danni. Could do without the ugly Northener but you can always kip through his bits.

2.35 GOOD IDEAS OF THE 20th CENTURY: The Female Orgasm: it would be an even better idea to show one but even at this hour fat chance. Probably better off going to bed and trying to conjure one up for yourself.

2.50 FILM: Who's Afraid of Virginia Woolf. Who's even heard of Virginia Woolf?

4.20 CLOSE DOWN: Wonder what they do? Pick dirty bits out of DH Lawrence novels? Jim Jam time.

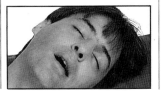

ITV

7.00 EMMERDALE (T): Formerly Emmerdale Farm, of course. Not many programmes change their name. 'Yes, Minister' becoming 'Yes, Prime Minister' is the only one we could think of.

7.30 CELEBRITY SQUARES: Comedy quiz with Bob Monkhouse and probably Frank Bruno.

8.00 THE BILL (T) (S) (Q): Lots of people shouting.

8.30 WORLD IN ACTION: Young, Gifted and Topless. See best documentary.

9.00 INTERNATIONAL ATHLETICS (TT): Live from somewhere or other. All the men commentators will be trying hard not to say "Bloody hell, look at that Italian sprinter in that leotard, it shouldn't be allowed" and "Well, I wouldn't mind giving *that* a hop, step and a jump."

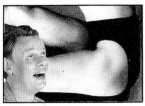

10.00 NEWS (T); WEATHER; REGIONAL NEWS.

10.40 FILM: The Graduate (TT). We think if Dustin has been a bit cannier he could have had Anne Bancroft during the weekday afternoons and Katherine Ross in the evenings and at weekends. It's great when they sit on the bus at the end smiling and looking all hot. Apparently Anne Bancroft is married to Mel Brooks.

12.30 QUIZ NIGHT: Pub quiz with Stewart Hall. We sometimes video this.

Totty trumps

TOTTY TRUMPS
Beth Jordache

Height: 5'5"   **Leg span:** 0.4m
Arse/eyes ratio: 8
Baps: 5
Known boyfriends: 0
Greatest asset: She's a lessie you can fancy.
Worst asset: She's dead.
Looks great wearing: Vanessa Paradis.
Maintenance Level: Low, just a few flowers on the grave on her birthday.

TOTTY TRUMPS
Vanessa Joe le Taxi

Height: 5'2"   **Leg span:** 0.3m
Arse/eyes ratio: 2   **Baps:** 7.5
Known boyfriends: 2 (some taxi driver called Joe & Lenny Kravitz)
Greatest asset: Childlike elfin innocence combined with knowing French sexuality.
Worst asset: Lives in Paris. Only goes out with taxi drivers and pop stars who think they're Jimmy Hendrix.
Looks great wearing: Euro Disney mini Mouse jim-jams.
Maintenance Level: High, especially when exchange rates are low.

TOTTY TRUMPS
Divine Brown

Height: 6'3"   **Leg span:** 1.2m
Arse/eyes ratio: 1
Baps: 30 (did you see the piccies??).
Known boyfriends: 0.07 (the left-over bits of old Hugh).
Greatest asset: Unrepentant prossie.
Worst asset: Can look like a bloke in some photos.
Looks great wearing: Hugh Grant/Police identification number.
Maintenance Level: About $40 an hour.

TOTTY TRUMPS
Liz Hurley

Height: 5'6" **Leg span:** 0.5m

Arse/eyes ratio: 5

Baps: 8 (Real life), 10 (Film premieres).

Known boyfriends: 0.3 (there's not much left of old Hugh after the mauling she's given him).

Greatest asset: Leather dress with safety pins, ability to appeal to women journalists.

Worst asset: Acting ability.

Looks great wearing: Sulky pout of the Wronged Woman.

Maintenance Level: Low, disguised as very high. Quite happy to live in small flat in Earls Court.

TOTTY TRUMPS
The Queen

Height: 5'6" **Leg span:** 1m

Arse/eyes ratio: 0.5m

Baps: 12 (you never know who's reading this).

Known boyfriends: 1

Greatest asset: Britain.

Worst asset: Royal children, dodgy dress sense.

Looks great wearing: Crown, silk-print head scarfs, handcuffs.

Maintenance Level: High, never carries money so it would always be your round.

TOTTY TRUMPS
Claudia Schiffer

Height: 6'0" **Leg span:** 2.9m

Arse/eyes ratio: 46

Baps: No one number can do them justice.

Known boyfriends: 1 (some friend of Paul Daniels who's got the same name as a Dickens novel).

Greatest asset: Ability to look like she's made totally out of plastic.

Worst asset: Speaks like a MTV presenter. Thinks tennis players jokes are genuinely funny.

Looks great wearing: Cellophane.

Maintenance Level: High, would have to learn to make jumbo jet disappear on a daily basis before she would even think of shagging you.

TELEPHONES

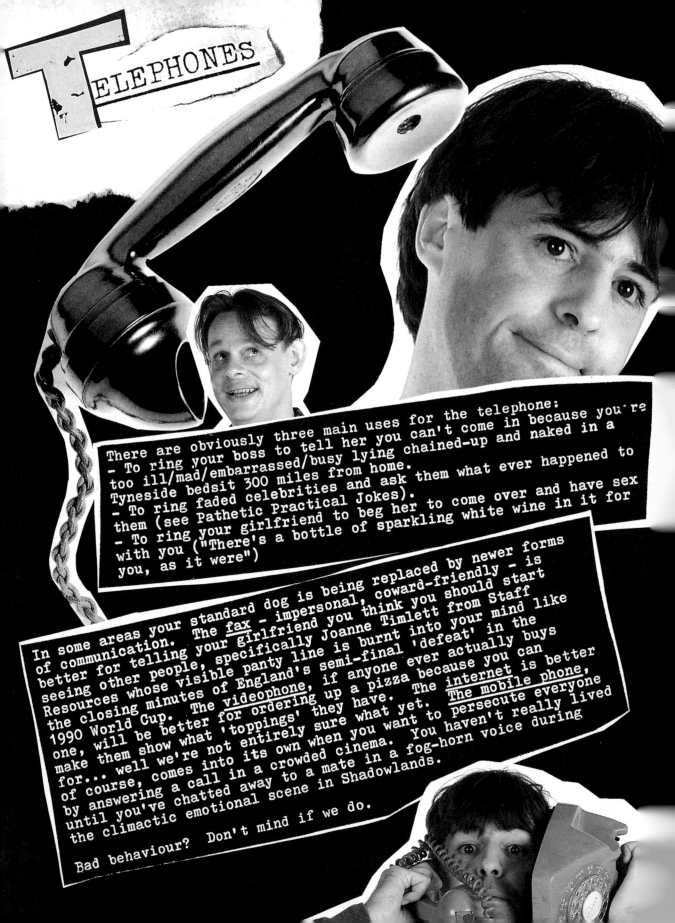

There are obviously three main uses for the telephone:
- To ring your boss to tell her you can't come in because you're too ill/mad/embarrassed/busy lying chained-up and naked in a Tyneside bedsit 300 miles from home.
- To ring faded celebrities and ask them what ever happened to them (see Pathetic Practical Jokes).
- To ring your girlfriend to beg her to come over and have sex with you ("There's a bottle of sparkling white wine in it for you, as it were")

In some areas your standard dog is being replaced by newer forms of communication. The <u>fax</u> - impersonal, coward-friendly - is better for telling your girlfriend you think you should start seeing other people, specifically Joanne Timlett from Staff Resources whose visible panty line is burnt into your mind like the closing minutes of England's semi-final 'defeat' in the 1990 World Cup. The <u>videophone</u>, if anyone ever actually buys one, will be better for ordering up a pizza because you can make them show what 'toppings' they have. The <u>internet</u> is better for... well we're not entirely sure what yet. <u>The mobile phone</u>, of course, comes into its own when you want to persecute everyone by answering a call in a crowded cinema. You haven't really lived until you've chatted away to a mate in a fog-horn voice during the climactic emotional scene in Shadowlands.

Bad behaviour? Don't mind if we do.

THINGS TO STEAL ON THE WAY HOME FROM THE PUB

1.   Door of pub
2.   Bill Oddie's front gate
3.   Letter 'T' out of a Boots sign
4.   Gravel
5.   Roadsigns, especially "Horses Crossing"

6.   The bumper off Simon Le Bon's Vauxhall Astra
7.   Garden gnome, especially if fishing

8.   Simon Le Bon's house
9.   Minor Girls Public School
10. Simon Le Bon's wife, Yasmin

UNDERWEAR, Impressions with.

Ask yourself this. Why is it that you never see a hat and think you want to put your bollocks in it, but put a bloke alone in a room with a pair of pants and a mirror and you just <u>know</u> that - sooner or later (sooner, if he's also got a six-pack) - he's going to try wearing those shreddies on his head. And very funny it'll look too.

However, few go on to exploit the full pants potential, which is a pity as - with access to just a few additional common items of male and female underwear - the opportunity for making yourself look a complete pillock is enormous.

Here are just some of our favourites:

TOP SURGEON

LAWRENCE OF ARABIA

PIRATE

S.A.S SOLDIER

FEMALE GENITALIA

VERY BRIEF HISTORY OF LAGER

Not many people realise that lager is a British invention. Its first mention in recorded history dates back to Elizabethan times, when Sir Francis Drake refused to go and beat holy shit out of the Spanish Armada until he'd finished off his bowls, which is what lager was drunk out of in those days.

In the 17th century the Real Mead lobby fought back and lager sales took a tumble. Nobody really drank it after that until a then little-known politician Benjamin Disraeli started a Lager Club in the bowels of the House of Commons. Its popularity fuelled by the invention of crisps by Somerset solicitor Tom Crisp around that time, lager now became an unstoppable force. It was becoming acceptable for women too, especially after Queen Victoria was photographed ordering a lager shandy in a Windsor hostelry in 1888.

During the last war lager was severely rationed so people tried to brew their own out of whatever odds and ends they could grow in the garden. But they quickly discovered that you need hops really.

During Prohibition in America lager became very scarce. A single bottle, drunk in secret in illicit Drinkeasies, had to be shared among up to fifty people, each of them taking a sip then passing it on. Hence the expression "Don't gob in it."

VIRGINITY

Although we secretly admire men who lost their virginity while they were still young enough to get a half fare on a bus, we are going to exercise some responsibility here and say: You are not necessarily a worse bloke if you wait until you are sixteen.

Nobody we know has ever slept with a virgin. We think one guy's going around doing it all.

Perfect Woman

Some people have the odd idea that there is no such thing as the Perfect Woman and that Man's attempt to find her are as impossible as trying to write on water. Obviously these people haven't done what we've done and really tried to find Her by staying up the whole night with a dozen cans of Stella, a pair of scissors, a stack of magazines and a jar of U-Hu.

This is the result of our latest search. As you can see she is perfection herself which is what you would expect after an intense sifting and discussion process that lasted the best part of a whole year.

VOICE: ANNIE LENNOX. THERE IS SOMETHING ABOUT WOMEN WHO ALWAYS SOUND LIKE THEY HAVE GOT A COLD.

EYEBROWS: GABRIELLA SABATINI (OFF THE BOIL ELSEWHERE)
TIT (LEFT): KYLIE — SMALL BUT PERFECTLY FORMED. LOOKS GREAT WITH WAVES LAPPING ON IT. TIT (RIGHT): ELLE McPHERSON — OUTSTANDING.

LEGS: STEFFI GRAFF — LIKE A GAZELLE'S THAT'S BEEN GONE OVER A COUPLE OF TIMES WITH A LADY-SHAVE.

HAIR: BJÖRKS — IMAGINE THE HOURS OF FUN YOU COULD HAVE UNDOING HER BEADING WHILE SHE'S ASLEEP.
EYES: WINONA RYDER. SO GOOD WE DECIDED TO HAVE BOTH.
NOSE: NICOLE FROM RENAULT CLIO AD. SHE'D TURN THIS UP AT ANYTHING.

BELLY BUTTON: KYLIE. SOME THINGS DON'T NEED EXPLAINING.

Why don't you and one of your mates do one of these for yourselves? This will help you clarify your latest thinking on all sorts of vital issues such as the perfect lip size, leg texture and eyes to arse ratios. You'll also have an instant guide to what you're really looking for in a bird which can be pulled out whenever you meet someone new and need to decide there and then if she's really worth lavishing money and/or your best funniest drinking stories on.

WARNING!!!!!!! Finding the perfect girl is not an easy job and you should be prepared for a long haul if you're going to get anything like a decent result. While engaged on your search though, try not to get so fussy that you never cop off with anyone at all.

Wrinklies

Let's face it. We all like having the odd cheap laugh at the expense of our elders and betters. One of our favourites (apart from using the word 'Pops' to perfectly fit men in their sixties) is sitting behind a couple of wannabee Victor Meldrews and describing in intimate but tasteful detail a sexual act that you just _know_ wasn't even invented when they were young.

Even more fun though can be had through the letters pages of the newspapers which, to the subtle mind, can provide the richest of pickings for harmless fun. All you need to do is write in using a suitably wrinkly name like Ernest Strong or Wally Hibbs asking the paper's older readers if anyone remembers a certain person or event from the long distant past.

For weeks after you'll be delighted to find the pages groaning with extraordinarily detailed reminiscences about the entirely fictional event you invented after a couple of lagers and a Findus thin crust Pizza. Particularily promising areas to ask your fellow readers for help with include: radio comedians of the mid-thirties, various obscure items of domestic hardware, bizarre apprenticeship rituals and harvest festival events involving the rolling of a whole Wenslydale cheese down a local hill.

If you should suffer any pangs of guilt when scores of lonely pensioners write in with stories of how They Were the Apprentice In the Barrel comfort yourself with the thought that letter-writing provides useful hand exercise for our older citizens and helps the time pass pleasantly enough till the Neighbours repeat comes on the television.

WHOOPEE CUSHION

If it's made of rubber and you can blow into it, chances are it figures prominently in the pantheon of Bad Behaviour i.e. condoms, water-bombs, three-hole dolls, and - last but not least - that Bladder of Delights, the whoopee cushion.

Inflated, this joke shop classic looks and feels alarmingly like a renegade implant from Miss Lusardi's chest, but just put it under someone and see the fun begin!

After prolonged discussion and debate, here are our Top Three Spots for the Old Rubber Rasberry-Maker:

1. **The State Opening of Parliament**
    To be slipped onto the Royal Throne by Black Rod - without the Queen seeing - just before Her Majesty sits down. In addition to provoking huge gales of laughter, this would also provide an ideal opportunity for satirical sketch writers with a "Seeing she's there to read out the Government's plans for the coming year, she's going comment. i.e. to be talking out of her backside anyway," etc.

2. **'In the Psychiatrist's Chair'**
    A chance to introduce a much-needed lighter note into this self-important Radio 4 psycho-babble egothon. Could also prove a useful diagnostic tool: Sitter/ subject laughs like a drain at sudden spurious trump- ing noise = good bloke, well-adjusted. Sitter/ subject shows silent indignation or complains = total neurotic fuck-up, keep away from ropes, sharp knives, strong lager, etc.

3. **Fifteen-to-One**
    The perfect way to humiliate first round losers even more. When they lose all three lives and master William G. Stewart asks them to 'Sit quiz- an unseen floor-manager nips in and places the Latex sit down in darkness, but for this new 'Whoopee Rag onto their seat. Normally contestants Cushion' version the lights would be left up so we could see them looking all embarrassed.

The sacking of Carol Vorderman from Tomorrow's World on a trumped-up Bad Behaviour charge has robbed the programme of much of its legendary up-front sexuality. Here was a TV presenter who'd clearly not only take you to several levels of ecstasy and back but could also leap out of the sack afterwards and fix your stereo using the latest micro-chips or what have you. Through the programme she would also probably have access to state-of-the-art contraceptive devices and creams.

THAT IS, UNTIL NOW

SHOULD BE IN THE SHOPS IN A YEAR OR TWO

The show's still worth watching though, especially when the demonstrations go wrong and the TW Team prove live to eight million couch potatoes that the revolutionary amphibious vehicle they're showing off about is complete rubbish. Unscheduled explosions are also good fun, especially when they make the presenters jump.

It's all very well them reporting on exciting bendy plastics and cures for diseases but what about something for the lads. Here are some inventions we would like to see:

- X-Ray specs. We're sorry but <u>why is this taking so long?</u>
- A gadget that automatically switches the TV off when Teresa Gorman or Brendan Foster are on screen.
- An early warning device for when you're about to dribble.
- The Virtual Reality Winona Ryder Holiday Companion.
- A gismo that gives a splitting headache to anyone who says "No actually I don't eat the flesh of dead animals".
- The Orgasmatron as featured in the film "Sleeper".
- A portable and user-friendly Lager Drip.
- Voice-activated condoms that unroll themselves on you when you murmer the words "Hang on a moment, they're here somewhere".

Xmas

The problem with Christmas - and you can slap us if we're not right on this one - is that it's not commercial enough. It used to be a no-messing, pants-off celebration of buying power. But increasingly people are moaning on and on about how as a nation perhaps we shouldn't be spending half our annual salary on pointless, ugly presents, food everybody is already too gob-stuffed to eat and booze that is turning the country's liver into a hideous shrivelled leathery thing. Are they mad?! That's the whole point! It's a party! It's a chance to go crazy! We need more chances to go crazy!

There are two kinds of Yuletide - with your family and with your mates.

Family Yule

Advantages:
* You over-indulged in the run-up and need access to a good first aid kit
* Your formerly troll-esque little niece has suddenly blossomed into Kate Moss
* Your Uncle Ralph shares with you his treasure chest of bad-taste jokes
* They have tree lights that flash on and off
* Your parents don't yet realise your life is a sham, full of sadness and broken dreams

Disadvantages:
* Everybody says you're looking more and more like Phil in Eastenders
* You have to keep shouting "Do you want a top-up?" at deaf elderly relatives
* Your niece probably won't go upstairs and play Adult Twister with you
* Your parents keep handing you your coat and saying "Bye, then"
* Uncle Ralph will insist on going upstairs to play Adult Twister with you

Mates Yule

Advantages:
* You can sit around for three or four days in your pants
* Nobody says "I know, let's turn the TV off and play a game!"
* Nobody says "Shh, the Queen's about to speak!"
* Nobody says "Must you drink Bailey's straight from the bottle?"
* Your Xmas morning listening is the boxed set "Live Shit" by Metallica

Disadvantages:
* You drink a litre bottle of egg nog at breakfast and sleep for 56 hours
* Someone vomits into the TV, is electro-cuted and has to go to Casualty
* The inflatable woman you bought goes down on you, but not in that sense
* Your gift to yourself is the worst hangover anybody has ever had, ever
* You are reminded that you don't actually have any mates

If you are one of those people who have trouble enjoying yourself at Christmas, let the follow-ing Bad Behaviour suggestions help you to perk things up a bit:

1.   Encourage your shy brother to perform his impression of Michael Barrymore, then stop him in the middle and say "I'm sorry, this is embarrassing."
2.   Gather everyone round, say you have a serious announcement to make and then collapse and pass out drunkenly for several hours.
3.   Ring up Noel Edmunds and say "Where's my present then?"
4.   After everyone has gone to bed, empty your bladder on the Christmas tree. When it turns yellow and crispy the next day, say knowledgeably "That'll be acid rain, of course."
5.   Threaten to shoot the family dog unless you are given custody of the TV remote control for the full Christmas period.
6.   Hum irritatingly during the Queen's Mess-age. Stop every time someone looks at you. Start again when they look away.
7.   Tell your very young nephews that Father Christmas not only doesn't exist but if he did, he'd hate and despise them.
8.   Instead of saying "Do you know, I'm going to cherish this lovely Gift Set of Honeys From Around The World for the rest of my life", say "Did you honestly think I'd like this?"
9.   Go round to Simon Le Bon's house and howl at the window until he or Yasmin give you some of their spare presents.
10. Surprise your family by offering to say grace at Christmas lunch.   Instead sing White Riot by The Clash.

YUCCA PLANT GAME

EXPLANATION.

Yucca plants are the kind of things birds give you when they're trying to turn your flat into their flat. Yucca plants must therefore be destroyed at all costs, as they are the first links in a chain which could bind you to one girl for the rest of your life. This game is a fun way of learning how to destroy a yucca plant in such a way as she will never know it was you that murdered it. All you need to play the game are two dice and nothing better to do.

THEY POST IT BACK TO YOU—
GO BACK FOUR SPACES

START

YOU TRY TO
FLUSH IT DOWN THE
TOILET, BUT IT BLOCKS
THE DRAIN —
GO BACK TWO SPACES

YOU POST
IT TO
SOMEONE—
GO FORWARD
THREE SPACES

YOU PUT
WEEDKILLER INTO
YOUR GIRLFRIEND'S
PLANT SPRAYER—
ROLL AGAIN

IN TRYING
TO STRANGLE
IT, YOU GET A
SPLINTER —
MISS A TURN

YOUNG LADS: Advice to youngsters

One of the great pleasures in life is leading a whole new generation into the light of proper Bad Behaviour. This is a heavy responsibility, so to help you answer those awkward questions from nephews, paper boys and school-kids at bus stops, we've compiled a handy guide of appropriate responses:

MY BUBBLE'S BIGGER THAN YOURS

Youngster: How can I prevent premature ejaculation?

You: It's best to think of a really disgusting image, such as a blubbery Nigel Lawson, his trousers wrapped round his ankles, humping a hippo. If that fails, you can always say to her, "I came what'S your problem?"

Youngster: Is there anything i can do to satisfy my growing sexual appetite?

You: No. You have to suffer in silence till you're 18 like the rest of us.

Youngster: What's a clitoris?

You: It's a new widget for canned lager. Nah, only kidding. It's the "GO!" button on a bird, except it isn't green or marked "GO!". That's why it's hard to find.

Youngster: And what's coitus interuptus?

You: That's when your mum barges in with some ironing while you're pulling your pud. Catholics say it's a mortal sin so remember: She's the one who should feel guilty.

Youngster: Is a long, thin one better than short fat one?

You: Depends on personal taste. Some blokes really go for porky birds.

Youngster: Can wanking be bad for you?

You: Only if you do it near an electric saw.

Youngster: Are love bites dangerous?

YOU: Only if they're below the waist and above the knee.

Youngster: What's the best sexual position to be in?

You: When she's gagging for it and willing to pay.

Youngster: What's a multiple orgasm?

You: That's when she has more than one orgasm a month. For some reason this is very rare.

Youngster: What's a G-spot?

You: A mythical spot devised by feminists to make us lads feel inadequate...I mean, try and make us feel inadequate.

Youngster: How long should an orgasm last?

You: For a girly, about 15 seconds. For a bloke, it's "Eeeoaaaaaarrghhh" about 3 seconds.

Youngster: When does a man reach his sexual peak?

You: On average, between the 4th and 5th pint.

ARSE

ZODIAC, ALTERNATIVE

ASDA
1st Jan - 16th Jan

Asdas are great consumers of more or less anything and your easy-going generosity can easily be mistaken for indiscriminate greed. Don't let this worry you. It's other people's problem that you buy life in bulk and don't mind throwing out the odd tomato along the way. Towards the end of the month use your spending power to get your own way and/or fill up on crisps and cola.

Famous Asdas include Pauline Quirk, Pauline Fowler, Jonathan Coleman and Gary Bushell.

NINTENDO
17th Jan - 21st March

Oh dear. You've done it again. Scarcely have you settled on one area of your life than you've moved onto another like a blue-arse fly on speed. Still, with your birth sign moving into the sign of Carling you should take the bumps smoothly enough. Life to you is a constant battle and no sooner have you defeated one enemy than another even more deadly one springs up. If you beat them without making lots of silly noises and going Powwww!!!! a lot of people might think you were less superficial. You can, after all, be a little wrapped up in yourself.

Famous Nintendos include Saddham Hussein, Madonna and Princess Diana.

CITRÔEN
22nd March - 23rd March

Here we go again. Your natural sense of style and sophistication has led you into a tricky situation with a less-fashion conscious colleague or elderly relative. Be careful of seeming too aloof. Citrôens can be arrogant and you should try to counter this by wearing trousers that are just too tight for you and moving to Ipswich. With full moon rising in Asda you would be unwise to do much more than sit in front of the telly with a bag of chili chips and a saucy late-night documentary.

Famous Citrôens: Thomas a Beckett, Thomas Dolby and the female cast of White Horses.

MICROSOFT™
24th March - 23rd May

Let's face it you're boiling over with ambition at the moment and you feel almost nothing can stop you in your quest for domination and control. The strain of constantly re-inventing yourself though is likely to tell when your ascendant enters into Hygena on the 13th when good old fashioned planning will be required to see you though. Don't get so absorbed in your work that you neglect your friends or your sex life. Money isn't everything.

Famous Microsofts™ include Sam Fox, Shirley McClean and Twiggy.

CARLING
24th May - 4th June

Beware. Though people look up to you pride can come before a fall and your painless progress up the social scale could be halted by an unexpected revelation. In classic Carling style you will probably want to switch off the mobile and try and sleep this one out. Watch out for complicated business contracts or sex games with strangers on the 23rd. They may be a good idea in principle but they can play merry hell with your bank balance.

Famous Carlings include Will Carling, Carling

MONDEO
5th June - 19th Sept

You seem to be slowly coming to the realisation that Life is passing you by and that your past achievements count for little in this fragile and fast-paced world. This is a good thing to realise. It's no good harking back to a golden age that probably never existed anyway. Re-vamp yourself, live in the here and now. And throw out anything that's brown and fawn in your wardrobe.

Famous Mondeos include John Major and nobody else of any note or consequence.

CLIO
19th Sept - 26th Sept

Family or domestic issues are demanding a lot of your attention but with the moon in Mondeo spanking the hell out of your solar chart you would be wise to ignore them and attach yourself to a bar-stool instead. There are, after all, only so many times you can "Really? Oh dear" in a sad voice without laughing. On the positive side this is now the time to ring the changes (remembering of course to reverse the charges). Like most Clios you are completely allergic to bees.

Famous Clios: None

TRINITRON
11th Nov - 20th Dec

Promotion or some other kind of good news at work is on the cards but whatever you do don't do the usual Trinitron trick and start lording it up before your new executive name badge has arrived. Look out for opportunities to expand your emotional horizons on the 15th when the move into Clio helps you discover it was the dark-haired one in ABBA you fancied the most all along.

Famous Trinitrons include Wayne Sleep, Normski and the Crystal Palace youth reserve team.

PSION
27th Sept - 10th Oct

Your reputation as a serial womaniser has taken a severe dent when it was revealed that all 45 of your valentine's cards were written by you with your left-hand. Never mind. Big puffy clouds on 20th should signify that the times are a-changing and you should take a trip to Boots pronto if you want to avoid embarrassing pauses. Like all Psions you tend to take Ronnie Corbett far too seriously.

Famous Psions include Dame Shirley Porter, Adam Ant and that fat bloke from the Virgin Radio ad.

ELECTROLUX
21st Dec - 28th Dec

Your solid, dependable qualities have stood you in good stead over the years but perhaps you should look to updating your image if you want your success to continue. People can sometimes rely on you too much and take your presence for granted. Don't let them. There's a storm brewing on the 7th. Don't get caught in it without a good water-proof mac.

Famous Elecroluxes include Gary Linnekar, Magnus Magnusson and Judith Chalmers.

SOLERO
10th Oct - 10th Nov

Your bright sunny nature has led people up the garden path again and it's time for you to show there's more to you than meets the eye. Don't overdo it, especially on the twelfth when an eclipse in Trinitron could lead you to box above your weight with disastrous consequences. Your taste for luxury will be amply satisfied on the 25th. Don't bite off more than you can chew. You'll only be sick

Famous Soleros include Hugh Grant, Sonya, Terence Stamp and Terence Trent-D'Arby.

HYGENA
29th Dec - 29th Dec

What a funny time this is. For the first time in years you've thrown off the shackles and discovered the true delight of being rude to your relatives and spending the weekend dressing up in women's clothes. Though you're feeling self-indulgent and plump with desire the conjunction of Pluto in Carling and a slight thigh strain means that you're probably better off locking the front door and dialling some 0898 numbers. For God's sake stop whining about the terrible price of battery-powered sex aids!

Famous Hygenas include Jesus Christ, the Dali Lama and Cilla.

We would like to express our deepest thanks to the following for their help and inspiration during the writing of this book. We really couldn't have done it without you.

Eva Budorova
Thandie Newton
Sharon Davies
Danii Minogue
Debbie Harry
Linda Lewis
Girl in Neutrogena ad
Daniella Westbrook
Holly Aird
Kirstie Allie
Phillipa Forester
Fiona Armstrong
Glynis Barber
Floella Benjamin
Gina Bellman
Amanda Donahoe
Patti Boulaye
Leah Bracknell
Nikki Brooks
Julia Ormonde
Sue Carpenter
Susan Day
Sandra Dickinson
Jill Elkenberry
Juliette Binoche - merci
Anna Ford
Emma Freud
Katarina Krabbe
Bella Freud
Esther Freud
Fiona Fullerton
Gill Gascoine
Mariel Hemmingway
Sandra Bullock - keep up the good work
Carol Vorderman
Caroline Quentin
Emily Lloyd
Marie Helvin
Bonnie Langford
Twiggy
Shelley Long
Julie Christie
Meg Tilly
Darina Gallicia
Margot Kidder
Kate Bush
Allie Byrne
Annabel Croft
Sinead Cusack
Imogen Stubbs
Lisa Anson
Sinead O'Connor
Letizia Dean
Nanci Griffith
Tori Amos - good hair

Lulu
Joanna Lumley
Louise Germaine
Charlotte Colman
Helena Kennedy QC
Hayley Mills
Claudia Stumpfl
Nanette Newman
Catherine Oxenberg
Susan Penhaligon
Kelly McGinss
Brownstone
Sandrine Bonnaire
Maggie Philbin
Nicola Mair
Chrissie Hynde - but no singing
Saskia Reeves
Jennifer Powell
Frances Barber
Priscilla Presley
Victoria Principal
Juliet Aubrey
Carol Royle
Lisa Bonet
Terry Sue Pratt
Jennifer Saunders
Joanne Whalley
Michaela Strachan
Meg Ryan
Dr Miriam Stoppard
Betty Boo
Tracy Ward
Emma Wray
Princess Diana
Princess Stephanie of Monoco
Princess Caroline of Monaco
Jamie Lee Curtis
Zoe Ball
Donna Summer
Norwegian netball squad
Annette Bening
Sherilyn Fenn
Goldie Hawn
Sarah Lam
Tatum O'Neal
Yasmin Le Bon
Sonia
Patsy Kensit
Dolores O'Riordan
The Luna De Miel Girl Dancers
k d lang
Cindy Lauper

Kara Noble
Jessica Lange
Diana Ross
Traci Lords
Evonne Cawley
Nastassia Kinski
Anke Huber
Jane Seymour - but no
  talking
Sharon Stone

Tara Fitzgerald
Demi Moore
Kelly Hunter
The cast of Home & Away
Gigi Fernandez
Florence Griffith Joyner
Irene Jacob
Cuban women's 4x100
  metres relay team
Dolly Parton
Michelle Pfeiffer